READING EXPERT

A 5-LEVEL READING COURSE for EFL Readers

1

KB013918

READING EXPERT *1*

Series Editor	Yoo-seung Shin
Project Editors	Mina Song, Hyobin Park, Yuna Kim
Writers	Patrick Ferraro, Keeran Murphy, Nathaniel Galletta
Design	Hyunah Song
Editorial Designer	In-sun Lee
Special Thanks to	Seung-pyo Han, Hoe-young Kim, Hey-won Nam

Copyright©2020 by NE Neungyule, Inc.

First Printing 5 January 2020

14th Printing 15 May 2024

ISBN   979-11-253-2927-5

Photo Credits

www.istockphoto.com

www.shutterstock.com

www.dreamstime.com

INTRODUCTION

Reading Expert is a five-level reading course for EFL readers, with special relevance for junior and senior high school students. They will acquire not only reading skills but also knowledge of various contemporary and academic topics.

FEATURES

Covering Current, Academic Topics: Topics ranging from real world issues to academic subjects are covered in an easy and interesting way so that junior and senior high school students can understand them. These subjects appeal to students and can hold their attention.

Expanding Knowledge: Each unit is composed of two articles under one topic heading. These articles will help students expand their knowledge of various topics, including social and academic issues.

Practicing Reading Skills: Reading comprehension checkups encourage the use of important reading skills. They can be used to evaluate and improve students' comprehension skills, such as identifying main ideas, specific details, and implied meanings.

Tackling Longer Passages: EFL junior and senior high school students often find it difficult to read long passages because they have not received much exposure to lengthy material. Interesting and well-developed passages customized for EFL students will help learners to approach longer passages with ease. Summarizing exercises will also help them understand the flow of long passages.

Test-Oriented Questions: Many comprehension checkup questions are similar to TOEFL questions. They will be a stepping stone in preparing students for English tests at school, as well as for official English language tests such as TOEFL.

LEVEL	GRADE	WORDS LIMITS	UNITS
Reading Expert 1	Low-Intermediate	230 - 270	15
Reading Expert 2	Intermediate	250 - 300	15
Reading Expert 3		270 - 330	15
Reading Expert 4	Low-Advanced	290 - 350	15
Reading Expert 5		300 - 370	15

TO THE **STUDENTS**

Why Is Reading Challenging?

It is a very challenging, sometimes painful, experience for EFL students to read English newspapers, magazines, or books. There are various reasons for this: the high level of vocabulary and sentence structure, a lack of background knowledge on the topic, and a need for certain reading skills.

Become an Expert Reader with Reading Expert!

Reading Expert is a five-level reading course that is intended to improve your reading abilities gradually. There are 4 areas of reading strategies you need to focus on to improve your reading abilities.

1. Vocabulary Skills

When you run into an unfamiliar word, try to continue reading. In many cases a couple of unfamiliar words will not prevent general understanding of a passage. If you think they are still a barrier to further reading, use context clues. If they also do not provide enough information, it will be necessary to use your Word Book or look up the "problem word" in a dictionary.

2. Paragraph Approach

A passage is a collection of paragraphs, and the main point of each paragraph is organized into the main idea of the passage. When you read a passage, try not to just focus on the meaning of each sentence: Keep asking yourself, "What is the main point of this paragraph?" Questions on the main point of a paragraph and summary exercises will help you stay focused.

3. Understanding Long Passages

Young EFL readers have often not been exposed to long passages (more than 200 words), and they may find such passages difficult to understand. Various reading skills will be needed to understand long passages: scanning, skimming, understanding the structure of the passage, etc. Reading comprehension questions and summary exercises cover these reading skills.

4. Knowledge of the Topic

Just like when you're reading in your native language, a lack of background knowledge can prevent you from understanding the topic. The Reading Expert course covers a variety of topics, including academic subjects, social issues, world culture, and more. If you are not familiar with the topic in question, try to search for relevant information in books or on the Internet.

TO THE **TEACHER**

Reading Expert is a five-level reading course written by EFL teachers who have years of experience in teaching EFL students. It is simple to use in a classroom and interesting enough to keep students' attention. Each level is composed of 15 units, and each unit has two readings. Each unit contains the following sections:

Before Reading

The WARM-UP QUESTION before each reading is intended to get students ready by relating the topic to their lives. You can also help students by introducing background knowledge or explaining difficult words.

Readings

There are two readings for every unit. Before having students read the text, explain to them some important reading skills, such as scanning and skimming. After reading the passage, they can listen to an MP3 audio recording. Each reading is followed by a WORD CHECK. Students can use this section to practice guessing the meanings of the key words and expressions in context. WORD FOCUS, which shows collocations, synonyms, and antonyms, is provided alongside the passages. It will familiarize students with some natural English expressions while increasing their range of English vocabulary.

Comprehension Checkups

Readings are also followed by comprehension checkup questions. These are intended to help students identify the MAIN IDEA or subject of the passage and understand DETAILS. Questions related to reading skills are sometimes included.

Summary

A SUMMARY is provided for each reading and it can take a number of different forms, such as a basic summary, a graphic organizer, a note-taking summary, etc. All of these forms are designed to improve students' ability to understand and summarize a passage. There are various ways to use this section, such as assigning it as homework or having the students complete it without referring to the reading. It tests whether students understand the text as a whole.

Word Review Test

Learning vocabulary is important for EFL readers. They need to review key words, expressions, and difficult or unfamiliar words. A WORD REVIEW TEST comes at the end of every two units and is intended to test students' vocabulary.

TABLE OF **CONTENTS**

		Reading Skills	

Dear Miss Ella,

I have a big problem! My neighbor is a girl named Nicole. She and I have been friends all our lives, and we hang out all the time. Everything was great until yesterday. We were walking home from school when Nicole told me that she is in love with me! She said she was too shy to tell me before. But I wish she had never told me. I think she is a cool girl, and I love to spend time with her. But, Miss Ella, I don't love her! I actually have a crush on another girl at school: Amy. How can I tell Nicole that I don't love her? I want us to remain friends.

Sincerely,

Tony

Dear Tony,

Wow. What a difficult problem you have! It sounds like Nicole has a big crush on you. When someone has a crush, he or she feels romantic, confused, and in pain all at once! It will hurt Nicole to find out that you don't love her back. That means you must be very gentle with her. My advice is to tell her that you don't want to ruin your friendship. Describe the fun you have had together, and make sure she knows how much you like her. But be very careful not to sound romantic. Make it clear that you want her to be your friend, not your girlfriend. Also, be careful not to say the name of the girl that you like. If Nicole hears you say it, her heart will break even more. Good luck, Tony!

Sincerely,

Miss Ella

SEND

Choose the correct words for the blanks from the highlighted words in the passage.

1. _____ a feeling of being hurt
2. _____ not comfortable talking to other people
3. _____ to feel intense attraction toward sb
4. _____ to spend time with another person
5. _____ to destroy; to cause sth to stop working properly

*sb: somebody / sth: something

MAIN IDEA

1   What is Tony's problem in the passage?

   a. He is too shy to find a girlfriend.

   b. He doesn't know how to make friends.

   c. He doesn't love the girl who is in love with him.

   d. He has a crush on a girl who lives in his neighborhood.

DETAILS

2   Who is Miss Ella supposed to be?

   a. student   b. trainer   c. patient   d. counselor

3   According to the passage, Tony wants to _____.

   a. make Nicole love him

   b. have a new friend

   c. keep his friendship with Nicole

   d. help Nicole to be more confident

4   According to Miss Ella, how does a person feel when he or she has a crush?

   _____

5   If Tony follows Miss Ella's advice, what is he UNLIKELY to do?

   a. be gentle with Nicole when he talks to her

   b. tell Nicole that he doesn't want her to be his girlfriend

   c. talk about the good times he has had with Nicole

   d. let Nicole know who he has a crush on

SUMMARY

6   Use the words in the box to fill in the blanks.

   | gently   feelings   remaining   confused   pain   ruining   romantic |

   Problem   Tony's friend, Nicole, has _____ for him. He enjoys hanging out with Nicole, but he is interested in someone else. How can he fix the situation without causing Nicole _____?

   Advice   Tony should _____ tell Nicole that he wants to remain friends but make sure she understands that he does not have _____ feelings for her. He should remind her of the fun they've had together. To avoid _____ the friendship, he must not say the name of the girl who he likes.

WARM-UP QUESTION   • What kind of activities do you do in your free time?

Did you know that your brain changes throughout your life? When you were a toddler, it was like a sponge that absorbed everything around you. At that time, your parents helped guide and shape your brain's development. Your teenage years are another important stage. And this time you have the opportunity to affect how it changes.

Scientists say that between the ages of 13 and 25 your brain goes through a process of _____(A)_____. The brain cells and nerve connections that are used the most become stronger, while those that are used the least die off. This is why it is important to take part in healthy activities during this time. For example, spending a lot of time practicing the violin strengthens the brain connections involved in learning music. But if you watch a lot of TV, that is what the brain will get used to. _____(B)_____, the part of the brain that is used for making judgments isn't completely developed yet. This means that teenagers usually act based on emotions and follow along with what their friends do, even if it is not good for them. This may help explain why some teenagers try smoking and drinking alcohol, although it does not excuse such actions.

You can stop yourself from making bad decisions if you know about the changes that are happening in your brain. Don't forget that what you do as a teenager can affect the rest of your life. Always think carefully before you act and try your best to make healthy choices!

WORD FOCUS

Collocations for
stage

the **early** *stages*
a **critical** *stage*
reach a *stage*
go through a *stage*

WORD CHECK

Choose the correct words for the blanks from the highlighted words in the passage.

1. _____ a young child who is learning to walk
2. _____ a link between two or more things
3. _____ to allow or permit sth, especially sth wrong
4. _____ to take in and understand with one's mind
5. _____ a decision based on information, beliefs, and opinions

1   **What is the best title for the passage?**

    a. How to Make Your Brain Healthy

    b. Mysteries of the Human Brain

    c. How the Teenage Brain Develops

    d. Brain Development at Various Ages

2   **What is the best word for blank (A)?**

    a. expansion   b. selection

    c. understanding   d. completion

3   **According to paragraph 2, why is it important to take part in healthy activities during teenage years?**

    _____

4   **What is the best expression for blank (B)?**

    a. As a result   b. In short

    c. For example   d. In addition

5   **Which is NOT true about the changes that happen in your brain as a teenager?**

    a. The brain begins to absorb everything around you.

    b. Some nerve connections in your brain get stronger.

    c. Some nerve connections in your brain disappear.

    d. The brain region that makes judgments is developing.

6   **Use the words in the box to fill in the blanks.**

rarely   chooses   development   completely   often   good   begins

Two of the most important stages of brain _____ occur when you are a toddler and during your teenage years. Between 13 and 25 years of age, your brain _____ nerve connections and makes them stronger. It selects the ones that are used the most _____. Meanwhile, the connections that are _____ used die off. Since the teenage brain isn't fully developed for making judgments, it is very important to put extra effort into making _____ decisions.

WARM-UP QUESTION • What equipment do we need when we go scuba diving?

The world under the sea is magical. It is amazing to see whales and colorful fish swim peacefully through the water. Jacques-Yves Cousteau was one of
5 the people who made it possible for us to explore this environment and its wonders. He was born in France in 1910 and had a lifelong fascination with swimming and observing the underwater world.

10 In 1943, Cousteau created the first aqualung with the help of French engineer Emile Gagnan. This device made it possible for people to _____(A)_____ for a long time without having to come up for air. Modern scuba diving developed from this invention. Cousteau also created a camera that could be used deep underwater, and he used it to film his first sea documentaries.

15 In addition, Cousteau explored a sunken Roman ship beneath the ocean with divers and scientists, which was the first underwater *archaeological research. He wanted to share everything he learned about the sea with others, so he started to write books and filmed a television series called *The Undersea World of Jacques Cousteau*. The show began in 1968 and ran for nine seasons. It brought the beauty of the underwater world into the
20 homes of millions of people.

Later in life, Jacques-Yves Cousteau started to worry about the damaging effects of human activity on ocean environments. In 1973, he started the Cousteau Society in order to bring people's attention to this important issue. Today, this society has more than 300,000 members who continue to work on protecting the world's oceans.

*archaeological: having to do with the study of history by looking at physical evidence

WORD FOCUS

🌐 Collocations for

issue

a **big** *issue*
a **major** *issue*
resolve an *issue*
raise an *issue*

WORD CHECK

Choose the correct words for the blanks from the highlighted words in the passage.

1. _____ to travel around an unknown place
2. _____ causing harm to sth
3. _____ a new useful creation
4. _____ a great interest in sb or sth
5. _____ located beneath water

1 **What is the best title for the passage?**
   a. The Foundation of the Cousteau Society
   b. How Ocean Documentaries Became So Popular
   c. Jacques-Yves Cousteau: A World-Famous Sailor
   d. Jacques-Yves Cousteau: The Father of Underwater Exploration

2 **What is the best expression for blank (A)?**
   a. swim faster
   b. stay underwater
   c. see more clearly
   d. float on the water

3 **In paragraph 4, what does this important issue refer to?**

_____

4 **Which is NOT true about Jacques-Yves Cousteau?**
   a. He invented a camera that worked underwater.
   b. He was part of the first underwater archaeological research team.
   c. He produced a TV series that many people enjoyed.
   d. He founded an organization to help people explore the underwater world.

5 **Use the words in the box to fill in the blanks.**

| continue | research | camera | discover | divers | inventors | dangers |

Jacques-Yves Cousteau helped us _____ the beauty of the underwater world. He was one of the _____ of the aqualung, from which modern scuba diving developed. In addition, he developed a special _____ that he used deep in the sea to make documentaries. Cousteau did underwater _____ and shared what he learned with the public through his books and a popular TV show. He also founded the Cousteau Society to help save ocean environments from the _____ of human activity.

Throughout history, many brave people have fought for human rights. Jane Addams was one of these people. Addams was born in 1860. She was part of a new generation of educated, independent American women. In 1888, she traveled to London, England, with a friend. They visited Toynbee Hall, which was a new kind of charity called a
5 "settlement house." It was set up in a poor neighborhood to help the people who lived there. The two women decided to bring the idea to the USA.

The next year, Addams and her friend **found**ed Hull House, the first settlement house in the USA. It was located in a poor part of Chicago and allowed educated women to share their knowledge and skills with the local people. Important services were also
10 provided, including English classes for immigrants and job training. Hull House also offered a community center, a gym, and an art gallery.

Next, Addams began focusing on ending child labor. At the time, many children were working in factories in unsafe conditions. In 1902, she co-founded a group that educated people about the negative effects of child labor. Addams believed that a balanced
15 education would make kids better citizens. So Hull House offered them a wide range of classes. Soon, childhood education became a requirement across the country.

In addition to helping people in need, Addams dedicated her life to world peace as well. After World War I began, 20 Addams started working for global peace by writing articles and giving speeches. As a result of her lifelong efforts, she became the first American woman to win the Nobel Peace Prize in 1931.

WORD CHECK

Choose the correct words for the blanks from the highlighted words in the passage.

1. _____ sth that is necessary or must be done
2. _____ having all parts of sth in good proportion
3. _____ a person who moves to a new country to live there
4. _____ work done to make products or provide services
5. _____ an organization that provides social services to local residents

READING SKILL

Identifying main ideas within paragraphs

Every paragraph contains a main idea. This idea outlines the basic point of a paragraph. The first or last sentence of a paragraph usually gives us the main idea.

MAIN IDEA

1 What is the best title for the passage?
a. A Woman's Efforts to Improve Society
b. Helping the Young Workers of Hull House
c. Jane Addams: An American Teacher in London
d. The First School to Give Children Job Training

DETAILS

2 According to the passage, Toynbee Hall was the place that _____.
a. gave information to travelers
b. helped poor people
c. lent neighbors money
d. was created by women

3 According to paragraph 2, what did Hull House allow educated women to do?

_____

4 Write T if the statement is true or F if it's false.
(1) Jane Addams helped educate not only immigrants but also children. _____
(2) In the 1800s, childhood education was an obligation in the USA. _____

5 Which is NOT a proper description of Jane Addams according to the passage?
a. an educated woman
b. a founder of Hull House
c. an immigrant to the USA
d. a Nobel Prize winner

SUMMARY

6 Match each main point to the correct paragraph in the passage.
(1) Paragraph 1 •　　• ⓐ Addams made efforts for peace and was recognized for her work.
(2) Paragraph 2 •　　• ⓑ Addams became interested in the settlement house.
(3) Paragraph 3 •　　• ⓒ Addams attempted to improve the lives of American kids.
(4) Paragraph 4 •　　• ⓓ The first settlement house was founded in the USA.

15

WORD REVIEW TEST

[1~4] Choose the word that is closest in meaning to the underlined word.

1. His condition got worse as he didn't follow the doctor's advice.
    a. selection   b. recommendation   c. collection   d. reservation

2. Dave couldn't hide his emotions about Sally.
    a. secrets   b. rumors   c. feelings   d. intentions

3. The media affects how people think about their appearance.
    a. reflects   b. ignores   c. determines   d. influences

4. Teachers always make sure their students finish their homework on time.
    a. announce   b. ensure   c. offer   d. prefer

[5~7] Connect the matching words in columns A and B.

A		B
5. feel •		• a. one's best
6. make •		• b. romantic
7. try •		• c. judgments

[8~11] Choose the best word to complete each sentence. (Change the form if needed.)

hang out   crush   absorb   strengthen   involve   shy

8. Her weakness is that she is too _____ with new people.

9. I like to _____ with Tina because we share common interests.

10. These exercises were developed to _____ the muscles in your arms.

11. Her high intelligence allows her to _____ facts quickly.

[12~15] Choose the correct word for each definition.

nerve   confused   excuse   careful   development   hurt

12. the process of growing or becoming more advanced:

13. trying not to make a mistake:

14. unable to understand what is happening:

15. a body part that sends signals to and from the brain:

[1~3] Choose the word that is closest in meaning to the underlined word.

1. The patients were <u>observed</u> for a month after surgery.
   - a. treated
   - b. invited
   - c. interviewed
   - d. monitored

2. The teacher helped Steven <u>continue</u> his education.
   - a. figure out
   - b. put off
   - c. carry on
   - d. give up

3. We <u>offer</u> an opportunity for you to experience the local culture.
   - a. settle
   - b. deprive
   - c. provide
   - d. require

[4~7] Connect the matching words in columns A and B.

A		B
4. dedicate •		• a. the Nobel Peace Prize
5. film •		• b. research
6. win •		• c. one's life
7. do •		• d. a television series

[8~11] Choose the best word to complete each sentence.

8. Building a library has been her _____ dream.
   - a. lifelong
   - b. balanced
   - c. damaging
   - d. archaeological

9. The Great Wall of China is one of the _____ of the world.
   - a. activities
   - b. environments
   - c. immigrants
   - d. wonders

10. A new sign was _____ on the side of the road to warn drivers.
    - a. set up
    - b. carried out
    - c. pulled out
    - d. brought about

11. Sarah is a(n) _____ person who doesn't rely on her parents.
    - a. global
    - b. negative
    - c. unsafe
    - d. independent

[12~15] Choose the correct word for each definition.

| generation | device | neighborhood | effect | requirement | charity |

12. a machine or piece of equipment that does a specific job:

13. something that is caused by actions or events:

14. a certain area of a town or city:

15. an organization that gives money, goods, or help to people:

ASK A DOCTOR

HOME   CONTACT   Q&A

WARM-UP QUESTION • Have you ever suffered from food poisoning?

Food poisoning is a type of illness that is caused by eating spoiled or contaminated food. Food poisoning can make people severely ill. Therefore, it is important to know about its symptoms and what we can do to prevent it.

5

Q What are the causes of food poisoning?

A Food poisoning is caused by bacteria or viruses in raw food or contaminated water. One common group of bacteria that causes food poisoning is Salmonella. Salmonella can be found in raw or undercooked meat, poultry, milk, and eggs. Another is a type of

10 bacteria called *vibrio vulnificus*. It is present in seawater and carried by raw seafood. Finally, norovirus can be found in unwashed produce and contaminated shellfish. You can also get norovirus through contact with an infected person. Although most bacteria that cause food poisoning are common in summer, norovirus is more common in winter.

Q What are the symptoms of food poisoning?

15 **A** Common symptoms of food poisoning include nausea, diarrhea, and vomiting. Other symptoms include stomachache, blurry vision, and dizziness. In most cases, food poisoning is mild. However, it can sometimes lead to severe dehydration for children and the elderly, who are relatively weak. Therefore, they may need to visit a hospital if symptoms occur.

20 **Q** _____ (A) _____

A First, wash your hands with warm, soapy water before and after handling food and keep all the utensils clean. Also, you should always refrigerate or freeze perishable food within two hours of purchasing. When cooking, always keep raw food separate from ready-to-eat food to prevent cross contamination. Lastly, be sure to cook your food

25 until it reaches a safe temperature.

WORD CHECK

Choose the correct words for the blanks from the highlighted words in the passage.

1. _____ able to spoil easily, especially if not refrigerated
2. _____ not extreme or harsh
3. _____ a condition that shows evidence of a disease
4. _____ birds raised on a farm for their meat or eggs
5. _____ an instrument used for cooking, such as a spoon or knife

1 What is the best title for the passage?

    a. Are Raw Foods Worth the Risk?

    b. Food Poisoning: Its History and How to Cure It

    c. Things to Know About Food Poisoning

    d. Children and the Elderly, Watch What You Eat!

2 Which of the following is NOT true according to the passage?

    a. You can get salmonella poisoning if you eat raw meat.

    b. Raw seafood can carry *vibrio vulnificus*.

    c. Norovirus can be passed from person to person.

    d. Norovirus poisoning most commonly happens in summer.

3 Which is NOT mentioned as a symptom of food poisoning?

    a. pain in stomach   b. inability to see clearly

    c. feeling dizzy   d. having a fever

4 Why do children and the elderly need to visit a hospital when they get food poisoning?

    _____

5 What is the best expression for blank (A)?

    a. How can food poisoning be treated?

    b. How serious can food poisoning be?

    c. How can food poisoning be prevented?

    d. How long does food poisoning last?

6 Use the words in the box to fill in the blanks.

| hands | perishable | contact | contaminated | temperature | vomiting | foods |

Food Poisoning

Causes	bacteria or viruses in raw food or _____ water
Symptoms	• common symptoms: nausea, diarrhea, and _____ • other symptoms: stomachache, blurry vision, and dizziness
Prevention	• Wash your _____ and all utensils. • Keep _____ foods refrigerated or frozen. • Place raw foods away from ready-to-eat foods. • Foods should be cooked to a safe _____.

In the late 19th century, almost all of the people from the poor Italian village of Roseto Valfortore moved to a town in the United States. This town was founded in the state of Pennsylvania in 1887 by Nicola Rosato, who called it Roseto after his hometown. The Italian immigrants who settled there were looking for a better life.

5 In the 1960s, a doctor named Stewart Wolf discovered something very surprising in Roseto. After doing a study on everyone who lived there, he found that they were generally much healthier than the rest of the country. The number of people in the town dying from heart disease was half the national average. In fact, almost no one younger than 55 years of age died of a heart attack. And the death rate from other causes was 35% 10 lower than the national average. Many people simply died of old age.

So, what was the Rosetans' secret? ⓐ Wolf's findings showed that it certainly wasn't their diet. ⓑ They ate a lot of fatty food and many were very overweight. ⓒ There was no clear medical explanation for why they were so healthy. ⓓ Thus, researchers concluded that the Rosetans' excellent health was caused by the town itself. It was a 15 closely connected community of families. Most children, parents, and grandparents lived under one roof, and everyone got involved in church, festivals, and social activities.

Scientists refer to this mysterious **influence** of family and social life on 20 health as the "Roseto Effect." It shows that _____ (A) _____ can help people reduce the everyday stresses that are bad for one's health.

WORD FOCUS

◁ Collocations for

influence

a **strong** *influence*
a **negative** *influence*
political *influence*
have *influence* on

WORD CHECK

Choose the correct words for the blanks from the highlighted words in the passage.

1. _____ the place where one was born and grew up
2. _____ unusual and hard to understand
3. _____ to go to a new place and live there for a long time
4. _____ being heavier than one should be
5. _____ to establish a settlement, town, or country

READING SKILL

Understanding the flow
In smoothly flowing writing, all the sentences are arranged in the right order. No sentences stray from the topic. So, when reading the passage, see if individual sentences connect smoothly. Pay special attention to the connections between words and pronouns.

MAIN IDEA

1 What is the passage mainly about?
a. reasons Rosetans moved to the US
b. how diet affected the lives of immigrants
c. how Italian food makes you healthy
d. the Roseto community's key to good health

DETAILS

2 According to paragraph 1, how did the town of Roseto get its name?

_____

3 Where would the following sentence best fit in paragraph 3?

In addition, they worked long hours in jobs that were very hard on their bodies.

4 What is the best expression for blank (A)?
a. changing life patterns
b. living far away from the city
c. having close connections with others
d. maintaining a strong sense of independence

5 Which is NOT true about the Rosetans according to the passage?
a. They were immigrants who settled in Pennsylvania.
b. Their rate of heart diseases was lower than the American average.
c. Many of them died of natural causes.
d. Their health had something to do with their diet.

SUMMARY

6 Match each topic to the correct paragraph in the passage.
(1) Paragraph 1 •   • ⓐ Wolf's study on the health of Rosetans
(2) Paragraph 2 •   • ⓑ the conclusion taken from the Rosetan example
(3) Paragraph 3 •   • ⓒ early history of the town of Roseto
(4) Paragraph 4 •   • ⓓ explanation for the cause of Rosetans' great health

WARM-UP QUESTION • Have you ever heard of 3D printing?

Can you imagine walking into your kitchen and producing any food you want simply by touching a screen? 3D printing may soon make this possible. 3D printers can produce almost any kind of item by building it layer by layer. Now scientists are using them to "print" foods such as chocolate and even meat. So how does it work?

3D food printing is actually quite simple. First you put the raw materials into the printer. These are the same for all foods. They are protein, *carbohydrates, and fat. Next you tell the printer what ratio to use. Then you wait while the printer produces the food. In this way, people can create foods according to their _____(A)_____. For example, an athlete could print high-protein pasta. Or a pregnant woman could print bread with extra vitamins. In addition, somebody with an allergy could tell the printer to leave out a certain ingredient.

3D food printing seems to offer many benefits. First, printing food could save time. Instead of cooking food, people could print it while doing other things. Second, printed food might taste better than **ordinary** food. That's because people could print food with customized flavors. Third, it will likely offer exciting possibilities for food design. As different textures and shapes become available, any design you want is possible. Finally, it could improve our health. By allowing people to easily replace the unhealthy ingredients in processed foods with healthier options, it has the potential to help provide a more nutritious diet. With so many advantages, 3D printing may change the future of the food industry completely.

*carbohydrate: a substance in bread, potatoes, and other foods that provides energy

WORD FOCUS

⊜ Synonyms for
ordinary

normal
typical
usual

WORD
CHECK

Choose the correct words for the blanks from the highlighted words in the passage.

1. _____ the feel of an object or substance
2. _____ having a baby in one's body
3. _____ a comparative relationship that uses numbers
4. _____ being in a pure state
5. _____ a food or substance that is used in making a certain dish

1 **What is the passage mainly about?**

a. the future of 3D printing

b. steps to making 3D food

c. problems with 3D food technology

d. the features of 3D food printing

2 **According to paragraph 1, how do 3D printers make an item?**

_____

3 **What is the best word for blank (A)?**

a. feelings　　　b. needs　　　c. abilities　　　d. gender

4 **Write T if the statement is true or F if it's false.**

(1) Protein, carbohydrates, and fat are the raw materials that make up food. _____

(2) 3D food printers are not recommended for people with allergies. _____

5 **Which is NOT mentioned as a benefit of 3D food printing?**

a. better taste　　　　　　　　　b. varied food design

c. saving money　　　　　　　　d. reduced health risks

6 **Use the words in the box to fill in the blanks.**

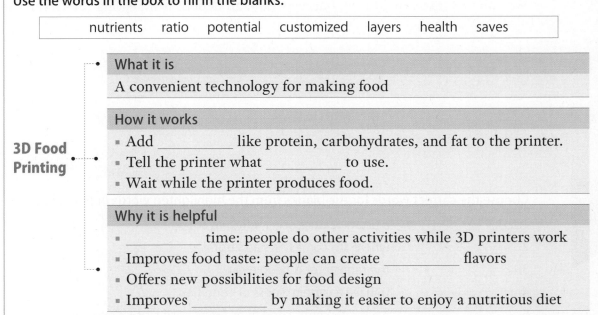

| nutrients   ratio   potential   customized   layers   health   saves |

3D Food Printing

What it is

A convenient technology for making food

How it works

- Add _____ like protein, carbohydrates, and fat to the printer.
- Tell the printer what _____ to use.
- Wait while the printer produces food.

Why it is helpful

- _____ time: people do other activities while 3D printers work
- Improves food taste: people can create _____ flavors
- Offers new possibilities for food design
- Improves _____ by making it easier to enjoy a nutritious diet

Like all national foods, those of Greece are a result of _____(A)_____ . There are three seas around Greece, so fresh fish is always available. The warm, dry climate is suitable for growing fruits and vegetables. Grapes can easily be grown in the sunshine. And the many olive trees are a source of olives. All of these natural factors give the people of Greece a very **healthy** diet.

Greek cooking uses many vegetables, which are an important source of vitamins. Therefore, it is not surprising that people who eat Greek food are likely to be healthy. Now scientists are finding out that certain vegetables can actually fight serious diseases. For example, tomatoes, which are commonly used in Greek dishes, help prevent certain types of cancer.

Traditional Greek food also fights another major killer: heart disease. Many Greek dishes use fish, which is good for people with high levels of cholesterol. Although some Greek dishes are very oily, very few Greeks suffer from heart disease. There seem to be two reasons for this. First, Greek people often drink a little red wine with meals, and scientists believe that this has advantages for fighting heart disease. Second, almost all Greek dishes are made using olive oil. This is one of the healthiest types of oil, full of vitamins and with no cholesterol.

Modern medical science offers great suggestions about healthy eating habits. But for hundreds of years, Greek people have been eating healthy foods that fight diseases. We can't all move to Greece, but we would all benefit from eating the Greek way.

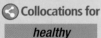

WORD FOCUS

◁ **Collocations for**

healthy

healthy **eating**
a *healthy* **lifestyle**
a *healthy* **appetite**
physically *healthy*

WORD CHECK

Choose the correct words for the blanks from the highlighted words in the passage.

1. _____ a useful feature or benefit that sth offers
2. _____ where sth comes or starts from
3. _____ the regular food people eat
4. _____ to have a certain illness or condition
5. _____ having the right conditions for a specific situation or purpose

Guessing unknown words in context

We often meet unknown words while reading a passage. At that time, context gives us an idea of the possible meaning. We can also use our knowledge of how a word is put together to work out its meaning.

MAIN IDEA

1 **What is the passage mainly about?**

a. healthy food all over the world

b. the healthiest diet in Greece

c. the most famous food in Greece

d. the healthiness of the Greek diet

DETAILS

2 **What is the best word for blank (A)?**

a. history   b. location   c. farming   d. tradition

3 **If something is available, you _____.**

a. can use it for free

b. can get, buy, or find it

c. cannot have enough of it

d. can use it unfairly

4 **Who is fish good for according to paragraph 3?**

_____

5 **According to the passage, which is NOT part of eating the Greek way?**

a. preparing dishes using many vegetables

b. eating fresh fish

c. drinking red wine with a meal

d. using a variety of cooking oils

SUMMARY

6 **Complete the main idea of each paragraph using words in the passage.**

- Paragraph 1: Because of their country's geographical position, the people of Greece have a very healthy _____.

- Paragraph 2: The _____ used in Greek food, such as tomatoes, have been shown to fight off certain diseases.

- Paragraph 3: Typical Greek dishes with fish, wine, and olive oil have _____ for preventing heart disease.

- Paragraph 4: Eating a Greek type of diet can help you stay _____.

WORD REVIEW TEST

[1~4] **Choose the word that is closest in meaning to the underlined word.**

1. Drinking <u>contaminated</u> water can make people sick.
   a. boiled   b. polluted   c. spilled   d. purified

2. The teammates felt a special <u>connection</u> by playing baseball together.
   a. hatred   b. memory   c. ability   d. bond

3. The studies have examined the <u>influence</u> of playing games on concentration.
   a. pressure   b. cause   c. effect   d. source

4. The door <u>prevented</u> the fire from spreading until the firefighters arrived.
   a. caused   b. kept   c. promoted   d. handled

[5~7] **Connect the matching words in columns A and B.**

A		B
5. work •		• a. bacteria
6. carry •		• b. one's hands
7. wash •		• c. long hours

[8~11] **Choose the best word to complete each sentence. (Change the form if needed.)**

settle   medical   refrigerate   mild   perishable   occur

8. He _____ in Canada a few years ago.

9. You need to _____ the milk before it goes bad.

10. _____ punishment has little effect on drunk driving.

11. I take a _____ check-up once a year.

[12~15] **Choose the correct word for each definition.**

average   present   conclude   separate   include   blurry

12. not joined to or touching something else:

13. to come to a decision about something:

14. the typical level or amount of something:

15. difficult to see something clearly:

[1~4] Choose the word that is closest in meaning to the underlined word.

1. A massive amount of information is <u>available</u> online.
   a. necessary   b. enjoyable   c. accessible   d. valuable

2. One of the <u>benefits</u> that the Internet offers is real-time updates.
   a. advantages   b. results   c. gifts   d. services

3. People who tell a lie <u>are likely</u> to do it again.
   a. want to   b. force to   c. have to   d. tend to

4. This exercise is <u>suitable</u> for both children and the elderly.
   a. popular   b. appropriate   c. common   d. attractive

[5~7] Connect the matching words in columns A and B.

A	B
5. make •	• a. heart disease
6. grow •	• b. dishes
7. suffer from •	• c. vegetables

[8~11] Choose the best word to complete each sentence. (Change the form if needed.)

factor   layer   serious   allergy   ratio   raw

8. Smoking is a major risk _____ for lung cancer.

9. The skin is composed of three different _____.

10. Her dinner is usually rice and _____ vegetables.

11. I have a severe _____ to peanuts, so I avoid them.

[12~15] Choose the correct word for each definition.

ordinary   climate   athlete   create   source   leave out

12. without any special features:

13. not to include something:

14. the general weather of an area:

15. a person who plays sports:

WARM-UP QUESTION • What do you think a company can do to help society?

These days, many corporations are interested in Corporate Social Responsibility (CSR). CSR includes things like investing in communities and protecting the environment. Such activities improve the _____(A)_____ of both a company and its products. In turn, this can lead to increased _____(B)_____.

There are a number of ways companies can practice CSR. IBM, for example, is helping people participate in the World Community Grid. They have created a small
10 program for personal computers. Whenever the computer is not in use, the program donates its computing power to the World Community Grid supercomputer. This supercomputer assists with medical research that may lead to cures for serious diseases.

Then there is Starbucks. This business works together with nonprofit organizations to improve the lives of people living in communities that grow coffee. In Guatemala, for
15 example, Starbucks has teamed up with Save the Children to bring educational programs to remote villages.

Finally, some companies are created specifically to practice CSR. TOMS Shoes, founded by Blake Mycoskie, is one example. Mycoskie traveled through Argentina in 2006 and saw that many children had no shoes. Now, TOMS Shoes sells shoes all over
20 the world. For every pair they sell, they donate one pair to a child in a developing nation. They have now given away more than 35 million pairs of shoes worldwide.

CSR helps companies show consumers that they are not only making **profit**s but working to improve society. This makes the consumers more likely to choose products made by these companies. For these reasons, CSR is likely to expand in the future.

WORD FOCUS

◀ **Collocations for**

profit

turn a *profit*
maximize *profits*
a **huge** *profit*
a **handsome** *profit*

WORD CHECK

Choose the correct words for the blanks from the highlighted words in the passage.

1. _____ not having the purpose of making money
2. _____ to put money towards sth to help it grow
3. _____ sb who buys products or services
4. _____ located away from highly populated areas
5. _____ to give sth to help a person or organization

1 **What is the best title for the passage?**

   a. The Definition of CSR

   b. Companies Involved with CSR

   c. The Advantages and Disadvantages of CSR

   d. Corporate Employees Volunteering to Help Charities

2 **What is the best pair for blanks (A) and (B)?**

	(A)	(B)
a.	quality	tax cuts
b.	satisfaction	labor supply
c.	conditions	cost savings
d.	reputations	financial returns

3 **What does the supercomputer do with its extra power according to paragraph 2?**

_____

4 **What can be inferred from paragraphs 3 and 4?**

   a. Many coffee companies have been helped by Starbucks.

   b. Starbucks has some branches in remote parts of Guatemala.

   c. Blake Mycoskie is a well-known CEO in Argentina.

   d. A child can benefit when you buy a pair of shoes from TOMS Shoes.

5 **Use the words in the box to fill in the blanks.**

practice	connects	donates	profits	society	research	education

Topic	The number of companies practicing Corporate Social Responsibility (CSR) is increasing these days.
Examples	▪ IBM _____ people's computers to a medical research project. ▪ Starbucks works to help people in coffee-producing communities. ▪ TOMS Shoes _____ one pair of shoes for every pair it sells.
Benefits	▪ CSR improves a company's reputation and can lead to more _____. ▪ It creates better lives for people and improves _____.

Bookcrossing

There is an old saying, "If you love someone, set them free." Ron Hornbaker was a man who thought that this was true about books as well. He didn't want to see the books he loved become dusty on his shelf. He dreamed of sharing them with others. His goal was to "make the whole world a library" so that people could share their books for free.

5 Hornbaker wanted to encourage people to leave their books in public places for others to find. He decided to make this fun, so he started the website www.bookcrossing.com. Using this website, people can continue to enjoy a book by sharing it with others. Now the fun of reading doesn't end when the book does.

The process is a simple system called the "Three R's"—Read, Register, and Release. 10 First, someone reads a book. Next, he or she registers it on the website. The book is then given an ID number, which is put on the inside cover of the book. ■ Finally, the person releases the book by leaving it in a public place, such as a coffee shop or train station. ■ Once someone finds the book, he or she will hopefully go to the site to say that they have "caught it." ■ Then the "Three R's" start all over again. ■

15 When it was launched, about one hundred people joined the site per month. There are now over 950,000 members, and Bookcrossing books are making their way all over the world. Bookcrossing is a fun way to share your experience of reading with others.

1 According to the passage, Ron Hornbaker started Bookcrossing because

ⓐ people didn't read a lot of books

ⓑ there was no library in his town

ⓒ he wanted to share books with others

ⓓ it was difficult for him to find interesting books to read

2   The highlighted part in paragraph 2 means

   (a) people start to enjoy themselves when reading a book

   (b) Bookcrossing books are good to read

   (c) leaving a book in a public place is a fun thing to do

   (d) people can enjoy sharing their books with others

3   Look at the four squares [■] that indicate where the following sentence could be added to the passage.

This way, the original owner of the book can know that the book has been found.

Where would the sentence best fit?

4   All of the following are mentioned in paragraph 3 as part of the process of Bookcrossing EXCEPT

   (a) choosing a book and reading it

   (b) registering the book on the website

   (c) advertising the book on the website

   (d) leaving the book in a public place for others to find

5   The word launched in the passage is closest in meaning to

   (a) started   (b) updated   (c) designed   (d) ordered

6   Directions   Look at the sentence in bold. It is the first sentence of a short summary of the passage. Choose THREE answers to complete the summary. Wrong answer choices use minor ideas from the passage or use information that is not in the passage.

Ron Hornbaker created Bookcrossing.

   (a) Ron Hornbaker didn't like his old books.

   (b) People share books with others in a fun way.

   (c) Many celebrities are members of Bookcrossing.

   (d) Books are placed in public places so that someone can find them.

   (e) The website keeps track of the flow of books.

   (f) An ID number is necessary to enroll in Bookcrossing.

My Dear Theo,

I just received your warm letter. Thank you very much for the things you said. I am taking a rest today, so I have a chance to

5 write back.

You asked me about my paintings. As you know, I've always been interested in the special characteristics of each season. Well, it is autumn now, and the woods are showing unusual colors. I spent a whole day

10 sitting among the trees, admiring the beauty of nature. I tried to paint all the colors, but it was a difficult task. I used one and a half large tubes of white to paint the ground, even though it was very dark. I mixed the white with red, yellow, brown, and black. The result was a dark red, like the color of wine. There was also some fresh grass which caught the light and sparkled brightly. It was very difficult to paint.

15 I said to myself while I was doing it: I mustn't stop before I can show the mysterious mood of this autumn evening in my painting. However, because this light didn't last, I had to paint quickly, with a few strong touches of the brush.

I will continue to work as hard as I can. You asked about my health, but what about yours? I think my remedy would help you, too: to be outside, painting. Even

20 when I'm tired, I still feel like doing it.

I hope that you are happy and in good health.

Affectionately yours,
Vincent

WORD CHECK

Choose the correct words for the blanks from the highlighted words in the passage.

1. _____ to shine brightly because of reflected light
2. _____ sth that cures an illness or fixes a problem
3. _____ to want to do sth
4. _____ to remain; to continue to exist
5. _____ a special quality of sb or sth

MAIN IDEA

1 **What can we learn about Vincent from the letter?**
 a. how he learned to paint
 b. what he tried to paint outside
 c. how he succeeded as a painter
 d. what he wanted to paint in the future

READING SKILL

Identifying the purpose

Before you read, clearly identify your purpose for reading. By doing so, you can easily find what you are looking for, and you can ignore useless information. Identifying one's purpose helps one focus on important information and remember it better.

DETAILS

2 **What can be inferred about the painting mentioned in the passage?**
 a. Vincent painted it for Theo.
 b. It was painted with various colors.
 c. It is considered the best work of Vincent.
 d. It was Vincent's first painting about nature.

3 **Why did Vincent have to paint his picture of the autumn evening quickly?**

_____

4 **The underlined part especially reveals the painter's** _____.
 a. physical suffering
 b. passion for painting
 c. love for his brother
 d. ability to paint great pictures

5 **What remedy did Vincent suggest to Theo?**
 a. painting outside
 b. taking a good rest
 c. taking walks more often
 d. looking at the pictures he painted

SUMMARY

6 Use the words in the box to fill in the blanks.

| mixed season characteristics method admired touches light |

In his works, Vincent van Gogh showed the many _____ of autumn, especially the colors. He liked painting the variety of colors in nature. To do so, he _____ different colors of paint and found the perfect combinations. He had little time to work because the _____ did not last long in one place. Nevertheless, he felt like his _____ of working outside was good for his health and would benefit Theo too.

WARM-UP QUESTION • What is your favorite style of painting?

At the beginning of the 20th century, many artists started to move away from tradition. One of the modern art movements of this time was Fauvism, which started to develop in France in 1904. The term "Fauvism" comes from the French word *fauve*, which means "wild beasts." This name may have been chosen because Fauve artists

5 were viewed as rebels during their time. Their art shocked and even angered viewers. It took something that people considered "right" and made it look "wrong."

Henri Matisse was one of the founders of this movement. Along with other Fauve artists, he painted familiar forms in **color**s that didn't match them naturally. _____(A)_____, landscapes and portraits were painted in the "wrong" colors, which

10 were often bright and unusual. Traditionally, artists would choose a subject and paint it using its real-life colors. However, Matisse believed that form shouldn't decide color. Instead of simply making things look like they do in reality, he used colors in his paintings to express his feelings. As he put it, "When I put a green, it is not grass. When I put a blue, it is not the sky."

15 ⓐ The painting *Open Window, Collioure* is a great example of Matisse's use of color. ⓑ The scene doesn't seem natural because the water is a shade of pink, not blue, and the walls are different colors. ⓒ However, the colors express the excitement Matisse felt on a summer

20 day, which he wanted to recreate. ⓓ Like other Fauve artists, he believed that the colors an artist chooses are always right because they express the artist's creative visions.

WORD FOCUS

◀ Collocations for

color

a **light** *color*
a **vivid** *color*
mix *colors*
add *color* (to)

WORD CHECK

Choose the correct words for the blanks from the highlighted words in the passage.

1. _____ as existing in reality
2. _____ a large, dangerous wild animal
3. _____ one who opposes established ideas
4. _____ frequently seen or easily recognized
5. _____ to make sth exist or seem to exist again

MAIN IDEA

1 **What is the best title for the passage?**
   a. How to Choose Colors for Paintings
   b. Henri Matisse, a Leader of Fauvism
   c. The History of Fauvism in France
   d. Traditional vs. Modern Art Paintings

DETAILS

2 **Why was the term "Fauvism" chosen for the movement?**

_____

3 **What is the best expression for blank (A)?**
   a. Otherwise   b. In addition   c. In contrast   d. In other words

4 **According to paragraph 2, Matisse believed that** _____.
   a. artists should follow tradition
   b. it takes time to make choices about colors
   c. colors should be a means of expression
   d. colors should be chosen to represent reality

5 **Where would the following sentence best fit in paragraph 3?**

That is why Matisse didn't think there was any "right" or "wrong" when it comes to color.

SUMMARY

6 **Use the words in the box to fill in the blanks.**

express   right   unnatural   believed   movement   surprised   emotions

- **The development of Fauvism**
  - This modern art _____ began in France in 1904.
  - It _____ and angered people during its time.
- **Henri Matisse's Fauve art**
  - Matisse painted traditional subjects in _____ colors.
  - He chose colors that showed his _____.
- *Open Window, Collioure*
  - The painting's unusual colors _____ the feeling of excitement.

WORD REVIEW TEST

[1~4] Choose the word that is closest in meaning to the underlined word.

1. Sandra left for London to participate in a film festival.
    a. carry out   b. shut down   c. give a hand   d. take part in

2. We are training the dogs to assist blind people.
    a. help   b. please   c. love   d. follow

3. The investment has provided good returns.
    a. expectations   b. charges   c. reputations   d. profits

4. He released the fish he caught in the river.
    a. found out   b. let go   c. turned over   d. held up

[5~7] Connect the matching words in columns A and B.

A		B
5. protect •		• a. one's experience
6. set •		• b. the environment
7. share •		• c. them free

[8~11] Choose the best word to complete each sentence. (Change the form if needed.)

remote   educational   community   register   dusty   public

8. The apartment was _____ in my sister's name.

9. We rented a car due to the lack of _____ transportation in the area.

10. I found the website to be _____ and fun at the same time.

11. They are going to deliver medical supplies to _____ mountain areas.

[12~15] Choose the correct word for each definition.

nation   lead to   expand   organization   encourage   process

12. to grow in size, number or variety:

13. to motivate someone to do something:

14. a group of people who work together for a particular purpose:

15. a set of actions that someone takes to achieve a result:

[1~4] **Choose the word that is closest in meaning to the underlined word.**

1. He knows a good <u>remedy</u> for stomachaches.
    a. surgery   b. food   c. information   d. treatment

2. The sculpture was <u>viewed</u> as a failure by many people.
    a. left   b. sensed   c. proved   d. considered

3. My parents enjoyed the paintings of countryside <u>scenes</u> at the museum.
    a. sources   b. forms   c. settings   d. records

4. In the morning, we saw the surface of the lake <u>sparkling</u>.
    a. rising   b. moving   c. shining   d. changing

[5~7] **Connect the matching words in columns A and B.**

	A		B
5.	be in •		• a. a rest
6.	take •		• b. good health
7.	say to •		• c. oneself

[8~11] **Choose the best word to complete each sentence. (Change the form if needed.)**

reality   dark   chance   match   characteristic   familiar

8. She missed the last _____ to apply for the job.

9. Others saw her as confident, but in _____ she felt extremely nervous.

10. The place looked _____, though he had never been there before.

11. This lesson introduces the several _____ of successful people.

[12~15] **Choose the correct word for each definition.**

subject   admire   portrait   mood   modern   unusual

12. a painting, drawing, or photograph of someone:

13. relating to or belonging to the present time:

14. the main object of a work of art:

15. to think someone or something is impressive:

UNIT

07

Technology

READING 1

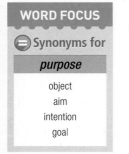

When you visit a website, you can see "http" or "https" at the beginning of your web browser's address bar. What do these letters mean? And what is their **purpose**? HTTP stands for

5 *hypertext transfer protocol. It is the standard way to exchange information between a web browser and a server. HTTP allows Internet users to access all kinds of content, including text, images, and videos. The problem is that using HTTP is not always safe. Other users can sneak into the browsing process and steal your valuable

10 information when HTTP is used. That's why HTTPS, a secure version, was created.

HTTPS makes web browsing safer by using secure encrypted connections between servers and browsers. Since other users cannot see the information that passes through these connections, HTTPS keeps your data private. _____(A)_____, HTTPS prevents hackers from replacing requested data with other, harmful data. The hackers also wouldn't

15 be able to steal the data since it is encrypted.

Because of its additional safety, most major websites are now using HTTPS. And popular web browsers like Google Chrome are encouraging this. Now, if a website uses HTTPS, Chrome shows a lock icon at the beginning of the web address bar to let you know that your information is safe. However, if a website uses HTTP, it displays a warning

20 message that says "not secure" instead. HTTPS is making the web safer, no matter what browser you use. So whenever you go online, make sure you see the "S"!

*hypertext: a software system that allows users to access information by clicking on a word or image

WORD FOCUS

⊜ Synonyms for

purpose

object
aim
intention
goal

WORD CHECK

Choose the correct words for the blanks from the highlighted words in the passage.

1. _____ to go somewhere secretly without being noticed
2. _____ to stop sth from happening
3. _____ normally used or accepted
4. _____ not open to other people or the public
5. _____ to rewrite certain data in a special code to make it secure

1 What is the best title for the passage?

a. A Safer Internet with HTTPS

b. Pros and Cons of Using HTTPS

c. The Reasons Hackers Prefer HTTP

d. Google Chrome vs. Other Web Browsers

2 Why is using HTTP not always safe?

_____

3 Write T if the statement is true or F if it's false.

(1) HTTP enables a web browser to exchange information with a server.   _____

(2) We cannot access our information because HTTP often encrypts data.   _____

4 What is the best expression for blank (A)?

a. However   b. Otherwise   c. In addition   d. As a result

5 What can be inferred from the passage?

a. HTTPS was created to increase Internet speed.

b. There are more HTTP websites than HTTPS websites as of now.

c. Hackers can't easily sneak into a website using HTTPS.

d. Chrome will warn you if you visit the website, "https://www.neungyule.com."

6 Choose the proper topic of each paragraph.

(1) Paragraph 1	ⓐ the meaning and function of HTTP
	ⓑ the differences between HTTP and HTTPS
(2) Paragraph 2	ⓐ how to upgrade HTTP to HTTPS
	ⓑ the benefits of using HTTPS
(3) Paragraph 3	ⓐ popularity of Google Chrome browser
	ⓑ the increasing use and promotion of HTTPS

U N I T
07
Technology

READING 2

What kind of knife isn't actually a knife?

The answer is the "CyberKnife." The CyberKnife Robotic Radiosurgery System is high-tech equipment being used by doctors to treat people with tumors.

After the tumor is located, the CyberKnife shoots beams of high-energy radiation that begin to destroy the tumor without hurting the patient. It is attached
5 to a robotic arm, which helps it automatically adjust to any movements the patient may make. It can be used on any part of the body, including the lungs, spine, and brain.

The CyberKnife is very accurate and can get rid of tumors without harming the surrounding tissue. This allows doctors to treat tumors in places that couldn't
10 be reached with traditional surgery. The tumors are not instantly removed, but the CyberKnife stops their growth and gradually reduces their size.

The recovery time of patients is also shorter with the CyberKnife. This makes it a good option for people who are too weak to undergo traditional kinds of surgery. It can be done quickly, with patients often going home the same day. All in all, it is
15 much less stressful than traditional surgery.

Tens of thousands of patients have already had their tumors treated in this fashion, with CyberKnife Robotic Radiosurgery Systems installed in hundreds of hospitals around the world. Cancer is a
20 difficult disease to overcome, but advanced technology like the CyberKnife is giving people hope.

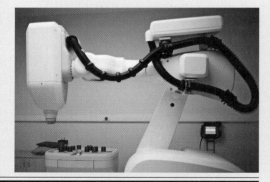

WORD CHECK

Choose the correct words for the blanks from the highlighted words in the passage.

1. _____ to find where sth or sb is
2. _____ part of a living thing made up of cells
3. _____ waves or rays of energy especially from nuclear reactions
4. _____ a mass of cells in the body that can cause illness
5. _____ to successfully handle sth despite difficulties

MAIN IDEA

1 **What is the passage mainly about?**

a. the risks of treating tumors

b. the danger of high-energy radiation

c. the effectiveness of traditional surgery

d. a leading-edge robotic surgery system

DETAILS

2 **Which is NOT mentioned as an advantage of using the CyberKnife?**

a. It adjusts to a patient's movements.

b. A tumor in any part of the body can be treated.

c. It doesn't harm tissue surrounding the tumor.

d. It costs less than traditional surgery.

3 **What makes the CyberKnife treatment a good option for weak people?**

_____

4 **What can be inferred about traditional surgery?**

a. It is less stressful for patients.

b. It has no serious side effects.

c. Its results are always clear immediately.

d. Patients need to stay in the hospital after the surgery.

5 **Which is closest in meaning to <u>fashion</u>?**

a. trend   b. manner   c. custom   d. tradition

SUMMARY

6 **Use the words in the box to fill in the blanks.**

| undergo   recovery   adjust   radiation   harm   surgery   growth |

CyberKnife Robotic Radiosurgery System

- locates the tumor → shoots it with _____ → doesn't _____ surrounding body parts
- doesn't instantly destroy tumors → stops their _____ → reduces their size
- is good for patients too weak for traditional _____
- can be done quickly and only requires a short _____ time

WARM-UP QUESTION • Do you know any animals whose blood is not red?

Horseshoe crabs are amazing creatures. They have barely changed in more than 250 million years. These days they provide scientists with a rare and valuable material: their blue blood.

5 Normal red blood contains iron, but horseshoe crab blood is blue because it contains copper. This, however, is not what makes their blood so useful. Instead, it is the way it clots. Clotting occurs when blood thickens and forms solid material. This is done to stop the flow of blood from a 10 cut or wound. Horseshoe crab blood begins to clot as soon as it encounters any type of impurity.

Frederick Bang, an American scientist, started experimenting with horseshoe crab blood in the 1950s. ⓐ He soon discovered the chemical that causes the clotting, known as Limulus amebocyte lysate, or LAL. ⓑ At that time, there wasn't a good **method** of 15 testing drugs for impurities. ⓒ Today, LAL is used in America to check all drugs before they are approved for human use. ⓓ

LAL is extremely rare and can cost as much as $15,000 per liter. A synthetic form of LAL, which can be produced without horseshoe crab blood, is now available. However, pharmaceutical companies have been slow to make the switch from the LAL found in 20 horseshoe crab blood. In order to preserve the species, scientists only extract about one third of the blood from each crab before returning it alive to the ocean. Despite this, thousands of horseshoe crabs are killed 25 during the blood-harvesting process each year. Hopefully, this number will decrease as synthetic LAL becomes more widely used.

WORD FOCUS

 Collocations for

method

an **effective** *method*
a **reliable** *method*
provide a *method*
develop a *method*

WORD CHECK

Choose the correct words for the blanks from the highlighted words in the passage.

1. _____ to become less, fewer, or lower in degree
2. _____ not common; hard to find
3. _____ a substance or flaw that prevents sth from being perfect
4. _____ a substance made of a specific type of molecule
5. _____ an injury, especially one that breaks the skin

1 **What is the passage mainly about?**

a. the health problems caused by blood clotting

b. the useful chemicals found in people's blood

c. the scientific value of horseshoe crab blood

d. the reason horseshoe crabs are endangered

2 **According to paragraph 2, when does horseshoe crab blood begin to clot?**

_____

3 **Where would the following sentence best fit in paragraph 3?**

But Bang realized that LAL could be used for this purpose.

4 **Which is closest in meaning to preserve?**

a. contain   b. protect   c. prevent   d. attract

5 **Which is NOT true about LAL according to the passage?**

a. An American scientist discovered it.

b. It is used to test drugs before human use.

c. Pharmaceutical companies are looking for ways to make it artificially.

d. Thousands of horseshoe crabs die in the process of extracting it.

6 **Use the words in the box to fill in the blanks.**

experiment   forms   drugs   clots   return   copper   obtain

The blue blood of horseshoe crabs quickly _____ in the presence of impurities. This is due to a chemical called LAL. A scientist named Frederick Bang found a use for LAL. He developed a process of using it to test _____ for impurities. Although synthetic LAL now exists, most companies still _____ LAL from horseshoe crab blood. Scientists take only one third of the blood from the crabs and _____ them to the ocean, but many still die during the process.

• What do you know about blood transfusions?

D o you know what a blood bank is for? It is not for saving money. It is for saving lives. If somebody has an accident and loses a lot of blood, doctors can help that person by giving him or her a blood transfusion.

5   It all sounds quite simple, but blood transfusions today are the result of over 300 years of experiments. In 1667, some British scientists **gather**ed to watch an experiment. A man had agreed to have some blood injected into his arm. The idea was similar to today's blood transfusions, but there was one important difference—the blood came from a sheep! This man survived, but another man died after a similar experiment in Paris. The doctor involved was nearly sent to jail for murder, and in 1678 the French government

10 stopped all blood transfusions.

    However, experiments with blood transfusions continued in Britain, and by 1840 doctors were carrying out human-to-human blood transfusions. But unfortunately these transfusions sometimes made people sicker. Finally, in 1901 an Austrian doctor named Karl Landsteiner discovered the reason for this—blood groups. He found out that there

15 are four main types of human blood: A, B, AB, and O. If a patient with blood type O needs a blood transfusion, doctors have to make sure the patient is given type O blood. Since this discovery, blood transfusions have been much safer and now save thousands of lives every year.

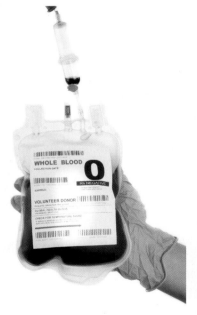

WORD FOCUS

⊜ Synonyms for

gather

assemble
congregate
flock
get together

*WORD
CHECK*

Choose the correct words for the blanks from the highlighted words in the passage.

1. _____ a place where criminals are put
2. _____ the act of putting blood into a body
3. _____ the crime of killing sb
4. _____ to continue to live
5. _____ to insert a substance into a body with a needle

READING SKILL

Identifying time order

Writers often use dates and times or other words to show the order of events — for example, "first," "next," "then," "later," "finally," and "today." These words can help you to understand a passage better. Read carefully and identify those words.

MAIN IDEA

1   **What is the passage mainly about?**

a. the danger of blood transfusions

b. the history of blood transfusions

c. the importance of blood transfusions

d. the difficulty of blood transfusions

DETAILS

2   **According to the passage, the blood transfusion experiment in 1667 was _____.**

a. human-to-animal   b. human-to-human

c. animal-to-animal   d. animal-to-human

3   **Write T if the statement is true or F if it's false.**

(1) Blood transfusions started over 300 years ago.   _____

(2) British scientists stopped experimenting with blood transfusions.   _____

(3) Blood groups were first discovered in sheep.   _____

(4) Karl Landsteiner's discovery made blood transfusions much safer.   _____

4   **Read the following sentences and put them in order.**

ⓐ Four types of human blood were found.

ⓑ Blood transfusions were banned in France.

ⓒ Doctors in Britain tried a human-to-human blood transfusion.

ⓓ British scientists injected blood from a sheep into a man's arm.

SUMMARY

5   **Use the words in the box to fill in the blanks.**

| types   safer   saved   sicker   continued   healthy   experimented |

Scientists in Britain and France _____ with blood transfusions in the 17th century. Sometimes the transfusions made people _____ and even killed them. However, research _____ and in 1901 an Austrian doctor named Karl Landsteiner discovered the fact that there are four main _____ of blood: A, B, AB, and O. Since that time, blood transfusions have been a lot _____.

WORD REVIEW TEST

[1~4] Choose the word that is closest in meaning to the underlined word.

1. Dona keeps her jewelry in a <u>secure</u> place.
   a. safe   b. private   c. wide   d. separate

2. The five stars of our logo <u>stand for</u> the five values of our company.
   a. introduce   b. destroy   c. sneak into   d. represent

3. The soldiers finally <u>located</u> their enemy hiding in the mountain.
   a. spotted   b. defeated   c. attacked   d. released

4. Tony usually goes jogging after work to <u>get rid of</u> stress.
   a. increase   b. control   c. cause   d. remove

[5~7] Connect the matching words in columns A and B.

A	B
5. shoot •	• a. a surgery
6. undergo •	• b. beams
7. exchange •	• c. information

[8~11] Choose the best word to complete each sentence. (Change the form if needed.)

hurt encourage access overcome connection replace

8. I checked the printer and _____ the used ink cartridge with a new one.

9. You need to enter a username and password to _____ the website.

10. I am sure that you can _____ the difficulties on your own.

11. Internet _____ in my house is unstable these days.

[12~15] Choose the correct word for each definition.

request steal recovery harm option content

12. to damage something:

13. one of the things that can be chosen in a particular situation:

14. the process of getting better after sickness or surgery:

15. to ask for something in a polite or formal way:

[1~4] Choose the word that is closest in meaning to the underlined word.

1. They discovered this beach while they were sailing around the island.
    a. saved   b. lost   c. found   d. involved

2. A survey is now being carried out worldwide.
    a. done   b. gathered   c. finished   d. agreed

3. The Mona Lisa is the most valuable painting in the museum.
    a. old   b. beautiful   c. popular   d. precious

4. I was so dizzy that I could barely walk last night.
    a. never   b. hardly   c. nearly   d. slowly

[5~7] Connect the matching words in columns A and B.

A	B
5. test •	• a. a life
6. save •	• b. solid material
7. form •	• c. a drug

[8~11] Choose the best word to complete each sentence. (Change the form if needed.)

> clot   transfusion   inject   encounter   survive   creature

8. Vitamin K helps your blood to _____ when you are bleeding.

9. Without water, no living thing could _____.

10. The patient seems to need a blood _____.

11. The nurse _____ a painkiller into my arm yesterday.

[12~15] Choose the correct word for each definition.

> experiment   synthetic   process   continue   involve   approve

12. a scientific study:

13. to officially allow something:

14. made from artificial substances:

15. to keep existing or happening without stopping:

Having started in 1877, the Championships, Wimbledon ("Wimbledon," for short) is the world's oldest tennis tournament. Today, it is one of the four "Grand Slam" tennis tournaments, along with the Australian Open, the French Open, and the US Open. However, Wimbledon is known as the most prestigious of them all. It is also known for a strict dress code.

For a long time, the Wimbledon dress code has required players to dress almost entirely in white. The tradition of wearing white while playing tennis can be traced back to the 1870s, when sweating was considered improper. Tennis players would wear white, which kept them cooler than other colors, so that they would _____(A)_____.

Many players have challenged the dress code. Former top-ranking player Andre Agassi, who liked colorful outfits, refused to play in the tournament from 1988 to 1990. Some other top players have been warned by officials for wearing colored garments and received media attention. Serena Williams wore brightly colored shorts under her skirt in 2010 and 2012. In 2013, Roger Federer was told to change his shoes because the soles were orange-colored!

In 2014, a very **specific** set of rules was introduced. These rules made it clear that, while non-white colors are allowed in a few places like the neckline and the sleeve cuff, only "a single trim of color no wider than one centimeter" is allowed. This rule also applies to headbands, socks, shoes, and even the players' underwear!

Wimbledon's dress code has been criticized for being too strict. However, the tournament's history and prestige help make it truly special. For this reason, the dress code is unlikely to change any time soon.

WORD FOCUS

↔ Antonyms for

specific

vague
ambiguous
fuzzy
imprecise

WORD
CHECK

Choose the correct words for the blanks from the highlighted words in the passage.

1. _____ completely or totally
2. _____ to go against sth like beliefs or rules
3. _____ not flexible
4. _____ not appropriate or right for a given situation
5. _____ a person who is in charge of enforcing the rules in a game

1 **What is the best title for the passage?**

    a. Wimbledon's Dress Code: The Tradition Lives On

    b. Wimbledon's Dress Code for Spectators

    c. White, the Most Appropriate Color for Tennis

    d. Wimbledon: The Most Fashionable Tournament

DETAILS

2 **Write T if the statement is true or F if it's false.**

    (1) Wimbledon is the oldest tennis tournament in the world.   _____

    (2) Wimbledon has required players to wear white since 2014.   _____

3 **What is the best expression for blank (A)?**

    a. breathe better   b. sweat less

    c. be seen well   d. look more attractive

4 **Why was Roger Federer told to change his shoes in 2013?**

_____

5 **According to the recent dress code, which would a player be allowed to wear in Wimbledon?**

    a. orange shoes with white-colored soles

    b. a black and white striped headband

    c. white socks with one centimeter wide red trim

    d. brightly colored underwear

SUMMARY

6 **Use the words in the box to fill in the blanks.**

colored	apply	improper	prestigious	allowable	change	white

- **The Championships, Wimbledon**

  - the world's oldest and most _____ tennis tournament

- **Wimbledon's dress code and the reason for it**

  - Players must dress almost entirely in _____.

  - Sweating was considered _____ in the 1870s.

- **The dress code today**

  - Specific rules were introduced in 2014.

  - unlikely to _____ in the near future

09

Sports

You might think that a Frisbee disc is just for tossing with your friends. But in many countries, it is used to play an exciting team sport called "Ultimate." Ultimate was created in the United States in the 1960s. But it has grown in popularity all over the world. Today, there are even many international championships held regularly.

Ultimate requires two teams of seven people each. And it is played on a rectangular field with an end-zone at both ends. Players pass the disc to their teammates in order to move it towards the other team's end-zone. The player holding the disc cannot run with it. Also, they must pass the disc swiftly to another player within ten seconds of catching it. When a player catches the disc inside the appropriate end-zone, his or her team earns one point. The game ends when one team reaches the predetermined number of points (usually 15).

One interesting aspect of Ultimate is its usual absence of referees. It is the players who call fouls and resolve any disagreements among themselves. Therefore, good sportsmanship is **essential**. All players must treat each other fairly and courteously. This environment of fairness and respect is known as the "Spirit of the Game."

In some cases, there is a mediator who watches the game and helps to make a decision if the two teams cannot resolve a disagreement. And some professional leagues do employ referees in order to prevent delays. But in every game of Ultimate, the most important thing is that the "Spirit of the Game" is upheld.

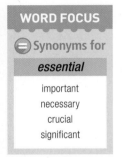

WORD FOCUS

Synonyms for
essential

important
necessary
crucial
significant

WORD CHECK

Choose the correct words for the blanks from the highlighted words in the passage.

1. _____ to handle a problem successfully
2. _____ fitting for the situation
3. _____ the degree to which a person, place, or thing is liked
4. _____ a situation where sth happens later than expected
5. _____ to throw carelessly or lightly

1 What is the passage mainly about?

    a. the rules and unique features of Ultimate

    b. the various leagues of Ultimate

    c. the meaning of the "Spirit of the Game"

    d. the reasons for Ultimate's growing popularity

2 Which is NOT mentioned about the rules of Ultimate?

    a. the number of players playing for each team

    b. the number of passes a team can make before scoring a goal

    c. the maximum number of seconds a player can hold the disc

    d. the number of points usually required to win the game

3 Which is closest in meaning to disagreements?

    a. questions   b. requirements   c. struggles   d. arguments

4 What does a mediator do during the game?

    _____

5 Which of the following is true according to the passage?

    a. A Frisbee disc was first created in the 1960s.

    b. There are two end-zones on the field of Ultimate.

    c. In Ultimate, players must run if they catch the disc.

    d. Referees are not employed in any Ultimate competitions.

6 Match each topic to the correct paragraph in the passage.

    (1) Paragraph 1 •   • ⓐ the rules of Ultimate

    (2) Paragraph 2 •   • ⓑ a unique feature of Ultimate

    (3) Paragraph 3 •   • ⓒ the sport known as Ultimate

    (4) Paragraph 4 •   • ⓓ the role of mediators and referees in Ultimate

WARM-UP QUESTION • Do you know which country Alaska belongs to?

Alaska is part of the United States, yet is separated from the mainland by Canada. Nevertheless, Alaska is the largest state in the US, one fifth the size of the rest of the country. The state is covered by huge glaciers and snow-topped mountains, including Mt. McKinley, the highest mountain in North

5 America. Thousands of tourists travel to Alaska each year to hike, hunt, and experience its great natural beauty.

10 Russian explorers discovered Alaska in 1741, and Russian fur traders soon began hunting in the sea around Alaska for *sea otters. They also built a few military forts and towns. However, Alaska was considered too far away for any Russians to live there. In the end, Russia sold Alaska to the United States in 1867. At a price of $7.2 million, the huge state cost only about two cents per acre.

15 _____(A)_____ its surprisingly low cost, many Americans thought that the purchase was a terrible **mistake**. Newspapers nicknamed the new area "Seward's Icebox" after the Secretary of State, William Henry Seward, who made the purchase. But later discoveries proved Alaska to be full of resources. When gold was discovered there in 20 1896, thousands moved there to get rich. The state is also a rich source of salmon, lumber, and oil, as well as an interesting place for tourists to visit. The state that was once called "Seward's Icebox" is now one of America's richest and 25 most beautiful places.

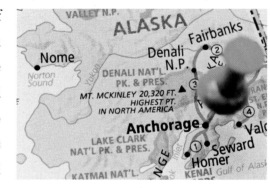

*sea otter: a large sea animal that lives around northern Pacific coasts, with very thick, dark brown fur

WORD FOCUS

🔗 **Collocations for**
mistake

a **silly** mistake
a **common** mistake
make a mistake
admit one's mistake

WORD CHECK

Choose the correct words for the blanks from the highlighted words in the passage.

1. _____ the act of buying sth
2. _____ a useful material existing in a country, which benefits its economy
3. _____ the covering of hair on an animal's skin
4. _____ to divide two things so that they are not touching each other
5. _____ a large body of ice found on mountains or moving down valleys

1 What is the best title for the passage?

a. Too Far Away to Live In
b. The Beautiful Nature of Alaska
c. The Richest "Icebox" in the US
d. The Coldest State of the US

2 Why did Russia sell Alaska to the United States?

_____

3 What is the best expression for blank (A)?

a. In spite of   b. Instead of
c. Thanks to   d. In addition to

4 How did Americans' thinking about Alaska change?

a. a wild land   →   a land of sea animals
b. a good tourist spot   →   a place for hunting
c. a bad purchase   →   a place of great resources
d. a source of wealth   →   a nice place to live

5 Which of the following is NOT mentioned in the passage?

a. a famous city in Alaska
b. the year Russia sold Alaska
c. the price the US paid for Alaska
d. natural resources discovered in Alaska

6 Use the words in the box to fill in the blanks.

difficulty	sold	useless	fur	resources	waste	largest

Alaska, a land of great natural beauty and the _____ state in the US, has an interesting history. Russian explorers discovered Alaska in the 18th century and used it for hunting. As Alaska was too far away from Russia, it was _____ to the US for only about two cents an acre. At the time, Americans thought it was a huge _____ of money, but history has shown that Alaska is full of _____.

The International Red Cross

In 1859, during the Second Italian War of Independence, the Battle of Solferino was fought in northern Italy. It lasted nine hours, and in the end, tens of thousands of soldiers were killed or wounded. This was far too many for the armies' medical teams to take care of. A Swiss businessman named Henry Dunant was traveling in the area when the battle
5 occurred, and he was horrified by the suffering of the soldiers.

A few years later he wrote a book about what he had seen. ■ In his book, he suggested that all armies should be accompanied by volunteer doctors and nurses who could help wounded soldiers from both sides. ■ The next year a Swiss organization called the Public Welfare Association held a meeting to discuss Dunant's proposal. ■ They set up
10 a committee of five members that included Dunant. ■

In 1864, representatives from European nations, Brazil, Mexico, and the US gathered in Switzerland to sign the "Geneva Convention for the *Amelioration of the Condition of the Wounded in Armies in the Field." It established rules that would allow Red Cross volunteers to enter battlefields without being harmed. Eventually these rules were accepted as
15 international law.

Due to a conflict with the group's leaders, Dunant was later kicked out of the organization. Despite being awarded the first Nobel Peace Prize in 1901, he was mostly forgotten when he died in 1910. However, the organization he started spread around the world. Today it has branches in nearly every country and more than 90 million employees
20 and volunteers work for the International Red Cross and its related organizations.

*amelioration: the act of improving a process or condition

1 What is the passage mainly about?

ⓐ the foundation of the International Red Cross

ⓑ criticisms surrounding the International Red Cross

ⓒ how an international organization works today

ⓓ reasons the Nobel Prize was awarded to Dunant

2 The word horrified in the passage is closest in meaning to

    ⓐ moved   ⓑ worried   ⓒ shocked   ⓓ delighted

3 Look at the four squares [■] that indicate where the following sentence could be added to the passage.

This committee was the beginning of the International Red Cross.

Where would the sentence best fit?

4 According to paragraph 3, the Geneva Convention

    ⓐ ended the Italian War completely

    ⓑ was approved by many different countries

    ⓒ helped Dunant receive the Nobel Peace Prize

    ⓓ sets the international rules for helping the poor during a war

5 According to the passage, Dunant was removed from the Red Cross because

    ⓐ he suffered from a severe illness

    ⓑ he had trouble with other leaders in the group

    ⓒ he disagreed with the rules established in 1864

    ⓓ he devoted himself to becoming a successful businessman

6   Directions   Look at the sentence in bold. It is the first sentence of a short summary of the passage. Choose THREE answers to complete the summary. Wrong answer choices use minor ideas from the passage or use information that is not in the passage.

Henry Dunant proposed wounded soldiers should be able to get help from medical volunteers.

    ⓐ The Battle of Solferino lasted nearly nine hours in northern Italy.

    ⓑ A Swiss organization discussed Dunant's ideas and created the Red Cross.

    ⓒ Various nations' representatives signed a document to protect Red Cross volunteers.

    ⓓ Dunant's reputation has finally been restored.

    ⓔ Henry Dunant won the Nobel Peace Prize in 1901.

    ⓕ The Red Cross and its related organizations have millions of employees and volunteers today.

WORD REVIEW TEST

[1~4] Choose the word that is closest in meaning to the underlined word.

1. Dona tossed the ball so high that I couldn't catch it.
    a. dropped   b. caught   c. threw   d. treated

2. This work doesn't require any special training or certification.
    a. reach   b. create   c. allow   d. demand

3. This traffic law applies to bicycles as well as cars.
    a. goes for   b. applies for   c. looks through d. fights with

4. Sam refused the job offer because he wanted some rest.
    a. rejected   b. employed   c. considered   d. criticized

[5~8] Connect the matching words in columns A and B.

A	B
5. play •	• a. a garment
6. resolve •	• b. a disagreement
7. wear •	• c. attention
8. receive •	• d. a team sport

[9~12] Choose the best word to complete each sentence. (Change the form if needed.)

fairness   interesting   improper   aspect   absence   strict

9. I will take care of your dog during your _____.

10. Some people questioned the _____ of the election.

11. We need to protect teenagers from _____ contents.

12. Buildings should be constructed under _____ safety standards.

[13~16] Choose the correct word for each definition.

essential   referee   disagreement   prestigious   warn   introduce

13. completely important and necessary:

14. respected by people for being important:

15. to bring up a plan or system for the first time:

16. a situation where people have different opinions about something:

[1~4] Choose the word that is closest in meaning to the underlined word.

1. He tried many jobs and became a writer <u>in the end</u>.
    a. soon   b. finally   c. suddenly   d. immediately

2. The police officer was <u>wounded</u> while chasing the criminal.
    a. saved   b. shocked   c. killed   d. injured

3. One of the best <u>discoveries</u> of the 20th century was penicillin.
    a. sources   b. findings   c. investments   d. records

4. His <u>proposal</u> was rejected because it was not realistic.
    a. dream   b. trust   c. agreement   d. suggestion

[5~7] Connect the matching words in columns A and B.

A		B
5. fight •		• a. rich
6. hold •		• b. a meeting
7. get •		• c. the battle

[8~11] Choose the best word to complete each sentence. (Change the form if needed.)

harm   resource   mainland   nickname   branch   conflict

8. Oil is a highly valuable natural _____.

9. A bridge to link the island to the _____ is under construction.

10. The company is planning to open a _____ in Boston.

11. Due to his aggressive attitude, people have _____ him "tiger."

[12~15] Choose the correct word for each definition.

explorer   accept   representative   state   fort   accompany

12. a place that is occupied by troops to defend the area:

13. someone who searches remote areas:

14. to go to a place with someone:

15. someone who speaks or makes decisions for someone else:

WARM-UP QUESTION • What do you know about Latin American music?

Music and dance play a big role in Latin American culture. The music is a mixture of traditional styles from the region's indigenous cultures, Europe, and Africa. It began when the Spanish brought stringed instruments and European music to the Americas. Later, African slaves brought drums and their own music.

5   Salsa is one of the most popular styles of Latin music, known for its fast tempo and **complex** rhythms. Salsa dancing, which involves moving your legs and hips to the beat of the lively music, is also popular. The origin of salsa can be found in Cuban music. After World War II, many Cubans moved to New York City. They settled in a neighborhood called Spanish Harlem. From there, their music mixed with that of other immigrants. By 10 the 1960s, modern salsa had been born.

    Another popular form of Latin music is samba. It originally developed in Brazil in the 19th century. Samba is played with stringed instruments, brass instruments and drums. Like salsa, it involves dancing as well. Traditional Brazilian samba dances are performed alone. However, ballroom samba, which is danced by couples, is more popular 15 in other countries. In the past, samba had a bad reputation due to the fact that it was often performed in poor neighborhoods. So people began to form clubs called "samba schools." These schools gained popularity as they performed samba dancing at festivals. Gradually, samba became a more respectable performance.

20   There are many other forms of Latin American music and dance. They include bossa nova, merengue, rumba, and tango. All of them are a blend of different cultures and are loved by people all around the world.

WORD FOCUS

⊜ Synonyms for

complex

complicated
intricate
sophisticated

WORD CHECK

Choose the correct words for the blanks from the highlighted words in the passage.

1. _____ to move to a new location and live there
2. _____ a mixture of two or more things
3. _____ the image or opinion that people have of sb or sth
4. _____ a device that is played to make music
5. _____ a person who isn't free and must obey and work for a master

Skimming

Skimming is looking quickly through the text to get a general idea of what it is about. We move our eyes quickly through the whole text, identifying the purpose of the passage or the main idea.

MAIN IDEA

1 What is the passage mainly about?

a. the origins of popular Latin American music and dances

b. the differences between salsa and samba

c. why Latin American music is closely connected to dancing

d. how African music and dancing spread to the Americas

DETAILS

2 According to paragraph 1, what did the Spanish people bring to the Americas?

_____

3 Which is NOT true about salsa and salsa dancing?

a. The tempo of salsa is fast.

b. Salsa dancing includes moving legs and hips.

c. The music of Cuba originated from salsa.

d. It wasn't until the 1960s that modern salsa appeared.

4 Samba's reputation was bad in the past because _____.

a. its rhythms were too complex

b. it was often played in poor areas

c. it was difficult to learn

d. people preferred dancing in pairs

5 Write T if the statement is true or F if it's false.

(1) It is ballroom samba that often features a solo dance. _____

(2) Samba schools improved the public perception of samba dancing. _____

SUMMARY

6 Use the words in the box to fill in the blanks.

beat   brass   complicated   drums   solo   settlers   slaves

Latin Music and Dance

A blend of cultures
• Latin America's indigenous cultures
• European cultures – stringed instruments brought by Spanish (1)_____
• African cultures – African music and (2)_____ introduced by slaves

Example 1: Salsa	Example 2: Samba
• Music – rapid tempo and (3)_____ rhythms	• Music – played with stringed instruments, brass, and drums
• Dance – moving legs and hips to the (4)_____	• Dance – traditionally a (5)_____ dance, sometimes performed by couples

You might think that parents have the right to choose any name for their children. However, this is not always the case. Many countries around the world have laws that regulate the naming of children. One of these countries is Denmark. Danish parents must choose a name from a government-approved list. The name must clearly show the gender of the child. It also must be spelled exactly as it appears on the list. Therefore, Danish parents can name their daughters Camilla, but Cammilla would not be allowed.

There is, however, a process that parents can follow if they want to _____(A)_____. They must start by getting approval from their local church. After that, the request is sent to the government. The government receives about 1,000 applications annually. But it rejects approximately 20% of them. Even if the name ends up being approved, the process can take months.

This policy may seem unfair and unnecessary. The government, however, has reasons for making it difficult to give children unusual names. The first reason is to protect the kids themselves. Children with strange names are often teased by their classmates. The other is to protect Denmark's cultural heritage. The country is trying to **preserve** the traditional names and spellings that have been used throughout Danish history.

Despite these reasons, many people oppose the policy. They believe it has a negative effect on diversity and fails to embrace the modern trend of globalism. In response, the Danish government has made the law less strict, increasing the number of names on the list from 7,000 names to 33,000.

WORD FOCUS

↔ Antonyms for

preserve

abandon
lose
destroy
ruin

WORD CHECK

Choose the correct words for the blanks from the highlighted words in the passage.

1. _____ a written request for sth, often made by filling out a form
2. _____ permission for or positive confirmation of an action
3. _____ the quality of being made up of many different types
4. _____ to control sth based on required or appropriate guidelines
5. _____ to make fun of sb by joking about them or annoying them

1   What is the best title for the passage?

   a. Difficulties of Making Strict Naming Laws
   b. The Unusual Origins of Some Danish Names
   c. An Easier Way to Choose a Name for Your Baby
   d. Denmark's Controversial Naming Regulations

DETAILS

2   What is the best expression for blank (A)?

   a. choose a typical Danish name   b. use a name that is not on the list
   c. use the most popular name   d. search for the government-approved list

3   Which is closest in meaning to heritage?

   a. artifact   b. legacy   c. antique   d. tribe

4   Why do many people oppose the naming policy in Denmark?

   _____

5   Which of the following is true according to the passage?

   a. Denmark is the only country that still has a strict naming law.
   b. The Danish government makes parents choose gender-neutral names.
   c. One purpose of the naming law in Denmark is to protect its culture.
   d. The Danish naming law hasn't been changed at all despite complaints.

SUMMARY

6   Use the words in the box to fill in the blanks.

   | church   history   gender   preserve   parents   government   embrace |

   Danish Naming Law

▪ Choosing baby names from those listed by (1) _____ - must clearly show the baby's (2) _____ - must follow the spelling rules on the list	▪ Choosing an unapproved name - must get (3) _____ approval first - must get government permission
▪ Reasons for the naming policy - to stop kids from getting teased - to (4) _____ Danish heritage	▪ Opinions and changes about the law - makes it difficult to (5) _____ diversity and globalism - has become less strict

• Have you ever watched an ASMR video?

Imagine fingernails tapping on a hard surface or drops of water falling into a puddle. How do these sounds make you feel? For many people, they create feelings of happiness and relaxation. This kind of experience is called ASMR. It stands for "autonomous sensory meridian response." People have been using it as a kind of therapy for years. They often record and listen to the sounds with high-tech equipment to **enhance** the effect. These days, it has become popular through free videos posted online.

People listening to ASMR sounds often report feeling a pleasurable tingle in their heads that travels down the backs of their necks. The sounds that create these feelings are called triggers. Some of the most common auditory ASMR triggers include whispering, scratching, or tapping on various surfaces. Along with sound triggers, there are also triggers related to sight and touch. In terms of visual triggers, repetitive hand movements are common. As to tactile triggers, playing with a toy slime is included. Some people respond to some triggers but not to others. And other people fail to respond at all.

People who respond to triggers use ASMR for various purposes. It can help people fall asleep or concentrate on their work. People also can feel less stressed and more relaxed. Even people suffering from depression can experience improvements in their moods after listening to ASMR.

Although interest in ASMR is growing rapidly, there still hasn't been enough scientific research to fully understand how it works. In the future, it is possible that mental health professionals will be able to use ASMR to treat some of their patients.

WORD FOCUS

Antonyms for

enhance

reduce
weaken
lessen

WORD CHECK

Choose the correct words for the blanks from the highlighted words in the passage.

1. _____ happening again and again
2. _____ sth that causes the start of a process
3. _____ acting or functioning independently
4. _____ to direct one's attention or effort toward one thing
5. _____ the machinery, tools, protective wear, etc. used in a specific activity

READING SKILL

Understanding the details

Details give readers a better explanation of what the author is trying to say. Details can be used to further describe the topic or to give examples. When dealing with detail questions, only use the information given in the text. Do not infer!

MAIN IDEA

1 What is the best title for the passage?

a. A New Way to Improve Your Listening Skills

b. The Pros and Cons of ASMR Therapy

c. The Potential Power of Sensory Reactions

d. Using All Your Senses to Learn Faster

DETAILS

2 Which is closest in meaning to <u>therapy</u>?

a. remedy   b. meditation   c. surgery   d. trick

3 What sensory responses do people report when listening to ASMR sounds?

_____

4 Which is NOT mentioned as a purpose of using ASMR?

a. to fall asleep

b. to enhance sensory abilities

c. to be more relaxed

d. to ease depression

5 Write T if the statement is true or F if it's false.

(1) Not only sounds but also visual signals can trigger ASMR. _____

(2) All people experience ASMR, but the triggers they respond to are different. _____

(3) How ASMR works has not been clearly revealed yet. _____

SUMMARY

6 Use the words in the box to fill in the blanks.

| depressed   popular   touching   relax   repeated   tingling   suffer |

ASMR

Definition	pleasurable feelings caused by certain triggers
Reaction	a _____ feeling in the head and neck's back area
Triggers	listening to sounds, watching _____ hand motions, and _____ objects
Uses	• to make it easier to fall asleep • to help stressed people _____ • to treat people who are _____

WARM-UP QUESTION • Are you a good decision-maker?

D o you find it difficult to decide what to wear when going out to meet your friends? Do you get stuck when you can't decide between two new smartphone models? If so, you might be struggling with indecisiveness.

Indecision can be a good thing when it prevents you from choosing without careful thought. However, if you hesitate too long, it can lead to frustration and missed opportunities. Indecisiveness is often caused by perfectionism. When people are too worried about making mistakes or the possibility of failure, they become unable to make any decision at all.

Luckily, there are some tips you can follow to avoid unnecessary hesitation. These tips will help you become a more confident decision-maker. First, following your intuition can be helpful. In order not to over-analyze, write down your options. And then quickly give each one a rating from one to ten. Then simply choose the option with the highest rating.

You can also practice your decision-making on trivial things, like what to eat for lunch. If you can get better at making quick, **firm** decisions on little things, you will be better equipped to tackle important decisions when you need to.

Finally, it can be helpful to acknowledge that many decisions aren't as important as they seem. Just ask yourself, "Will this decision matter in ten years?" Even if the answer is yes, remember that many decisions are reversible. For example, if you decide to enroll in an art class only to find that you don't enjoy it, you can just quit. The risk involved in trying something new is usually not that big.

WORD FOCUS

⊜ Synonyms for

firm

resolute
definite
determined

WORD CHECK

Choose the correct words for the blanks from the highlighted words in the passage.

1. _____ not doubting oneself
2. _____ to deal with a problem with determined effort
3. _____ to delay making a decision or waver between options
4. _____ the ability to know sth based on a feeling rather than facts
5. _____ able to be changed back or turned the opposite way

1 **What is the passage mainly about?**

   a. the positive and negative effects of indecisiveness

   b. strategies to help overcome indecisiveness

   c. the importance of making informed choices

   d. ways to avoid making wrong decisions

DETAILS

2 **According to paragraph 2, how can indecision help us?**

_____

3 **Why does the writer advise us to follow our intuition?**

   a. because it always leads us to correct answers

   b. because it prevents us from analyzing excessively

   c. because it allows us to enjoy the decision-making process

   d. because it is impossible to give a rating without intuition

4 **Which of the following is true according to the passage?**

   a. The more carefully you think, the better decisions you will make.

   b. People too afraid of failure are likely to experience indecisiveness.

   c. Making big decisions makes small decisions seem trivial.

   d. Most of the decisions are often difficult to cancel.

SUMMARY

5 Use the words in the box to fill in the blanks.

carefully	frustration	intuition	important	quickly	reversible	perfect

Indecisiveness

Advantage	It helps you think _____ before making a decision.
Disadvantage	It can lead to _____ and make people lose opportunities.
Cause	People can't make a decision easily when they feel they have to be _____.
Tips	▪ Follow your _____. ▪ Practice making small decisions. ▪ Accept that many decisions aren't that _____.

WORD REVIEW TEST

[1~4] Choose the word that is closest in meaning to the underlined word.

1. This national park was set up to preserve natural beauty of the area.
    a. conserve   b. form   c. break   d. tease

2. The leader tried to persuade the people who opposed the plan.
    a. overlooked   b. agreed   c. resisted   d. proposed

3. The festival is a perfect mixture of modern and traditional culture.
    a. blend   b. display   c. reminder   d. instrument

4. Some governments regulate the number of children a family can have.
    a. allow   b. control   c. choose   d. follow

[5~8] Connect the matching words in columns A and B.

A		B
5. move to •		• a. the lively music
6. play •		• b. an application
7. follow •		• c. a city
8. receive •		• d. a process

[9~12] Choose the best word to complete each sentence. (Change the form if needed.)

embrace   region   perform   unusual   diversity   approval

9. We try to respect the _____ of culture.

10. It is very _____ that this flower blooms in winter.

11. The band successfully _____ the show last night.

12. Almost all the houses in the _____ were destroyed by the flood.

[13~16] Choose the correct word for each definition.

origin   local   develop   involve   annually   complex

13. once every year:

14. the situation where something starts to exist:

15. to include something as a part of an activity or situation:

16. having lots of details and making something difficult:

[1~4] Choose the word that is closest in meaning to the underlined word.

1. Luke's <u>moods</u> have suddenly changed since he met her.
   a. feelings   b. movements   c. views   d. personalities

2. She knew by her <u>intuition</u> that something bad had happened.
   a. thought   b. intention   c. hesitation   d. instinct

3. The government is concerned with a lack of <u>professionals</u> in the IT industry.
   a. triggers   b. experts   c. opportunities   d. improvements

4. It is hard for me to <u>acknowledge</u> that my dog is dead.
   a. admit   b. report   c. decide   d. persuade

[5~8] Connect the matching words in columns A and B.

A		B
5. treat	• •	a. a patient
6. fall	• •	b. a surface
7. tap on	• •	c. a class
8. enroll in	• •	d. asleep

[9~12] Choose the best word to complete each sentence. (Change the form if needed.)

firm	include	struggle with	relaxed	equipment	frustration

9. I felt _____ with soft music and warm tea.

10. Your encouraging words turned _____ into hope.

11. The store sells cameras and related _____.

12. Roy is still _____ his science homework.

[13~16] Choose the correct word for each definition.

avoid	failure	experience	enhance	possibility	decision

13. to intensify or improve something:

14. not to do something wrong or unpleasant:

15. likelihood that something might occur:

16. a choice or judgment made after thinking:

UNIT 13

Animals

READING 1

When we think of birds, we usually picture them flying gracefully through the air. Not all birds can actually fly, but all birds have wings. However, wings are not unique to birds—insects and bats also have them. But what about feathers? All birds have feathers, and feathers are only found on birds.

Feathers are designed to be as light as possible. Yet they are also very strong and waterproof. If you look at a feather closely, you'll see that it is made of thousands of **tiny** parts. These parts are joined together in over a million places on a single feather. On a bird's wing, the feathers partly cover one another, so no air can pass through. This makes flight possible and keeps the bird warm.

But not all birds' feathers are the same. For example, albatrosses have strong, broad feathers that allow them to fly long distances. On the other hand, penguins have thick, oily feathers that keep them warm and dry while they swim in icy water.

Birds also use their feathers for a variety of other purposes. Some birds, for example, use their feathers to keep their eggs warm while they sit on them. And some have feathers that are the same color as their environment; this helps them hide from enemies. Other birds, such as the peacock, have very bright and colorful feathers, and they use them to attract a mate.

The feathers of all birds are different, depending on _____ (A) _____. While they are often beautiful, they are always essential to each bird species' survival.

WORD FOCUS

Synonyms for
tiny

small
little
minute

WORD CHECK

Choose the correct words for the blanks from the highlighted words in the passage.

1. _____ the length between two places
2. _____ movement through the air
3. _____ the reason sth is done or exists
4. _____ able to resist water
5. _____ to make sth or sb come to you by looking appealing

MAIN IDEA

1 What is the passage mainly about?

a. birds flying long distances

b. the various uses of birds' feathers by humans

c. the difference between bird species' wing sizes

d. the design and the purpose of birds' feathers

Scanning

When scanning, we rapidly search for the information we are looking for. The idea behind scanning is to locate specific information without reading through the entire passage. Even if you see a word that you don't understand, keep on going.

DETAILS

2 Which is NOT true about feathers according to the passage?

a. They are only found on birds.

b. They are very light and strong.

c. They are composed of many tiny parts.

d. They are arranged to let air pass through them.

3 What kind of feathers do penguins have?

_____

4 What is the best expression for blank (A)?

a. when they are born

b. what they usually eat

c. where and how they live

d. how they make their nests

SUMMARY

5 Use the words in the box to fill in the blanks.

connected	warmth	broad	colorful	waterproof	attract	picture

- **The special structure of feathers**
  - designed to be light, strong, and _____
  - thousands of small parts _____ together
- **Different kinds of birds, different kinds of feathers**
  - albatrosses: strong, _____ feathers for long flights
  - penguins: thick, oily feathers for _____ and dryness
- **Other functions of feathers**
  - keep birds' eggs warm
  - help birds hide from enemies
  - _____ mates

WILDLIFE

WARM-UP QUESTION • Have you ever seen a fish jump out of water?

A bird flying low over a lake may not think there is anything dangerous in the water. That is why it is surprised when a fish suddenly jumps out and catches it! Scientists recently discovered that this is what happens to barn swallows as they fly over the Schroda Dam lake in South Africa.

5 The fish that hunt these birds are African tigerfish. There are only about five types of freshwater fish in the world that feed on birds. Most of these fish only do this when a bird falls into the water or paddles on the surface right above them. African tigerfish, however, regularly hunt barn swallows. In fact, they do this every day. This may be because there isn't much other food for tigerfish to eat in the Schroda Dam 10 lake.

Scientists are amazed by the incredible hunting skills tigerfish have developed. When a tigerfish spots a barn swallow flying above the lake, it follows the bird by swimming near the surface or deeper in the water. It speeds up until it is going faster than the bird. Then it considers how the angle of light changes as the light enters the 15 water from the air. This allows the fish to be sure of the bird's actual position. Finally, the tigerfish jumps out of the water and grabs the barn swallow from the air with its sharp teeth.

This is the opposite of what happens in most food chains. Since it is much more common for birds to hunt fish, the fact that tigerfish feed on barn swallows is quite 20 extraordinary.

WORD CHECK

Choose the correct words for the blanks from the highlighted words in the passage.

1. _____ to eat sth to get nutrients
2. _____ to swim on the surface of water
3. _____ to aggressively take sth
4. _____ amazing; exceptional
5. _____ living in water that is not salty

MAIN IDEA

1   What is the best title for the passage?

  a. Tigerfish: Amazing Hunters of Birds

  b. Changes in Freshwater Food Chains

  c. The Clever Hunting Techniques of Barn Swallows

  d. The Decreasing Number of Tigerfish in South Africa

DETAILS

2   The writer suggests that the cause of the African tigerfish's rare behavior could be _____ .

  a. their use of the angle of light

  b. a lack of food available to them

  c. a lot of birds paddling on the water

  d. an increase in the number of barn swallows

3   Why does a tigerfish consider the changing angle of light when it hunts?

  _____

4   Why does the writer mention food chains in paragraph 4?

  a. to suggest that we need to clean up the Schroda Dam lake

  b. to show what kind of fish survive better in food chains

  c. to emphasize that the tigerfish's feeding habits are unusual

  d. to explain why tigerfish started to feed on birds

5   Which is NOT true about tigerfish according to the passage?

  a. They are found in a lake in South Africa.

  b. They are not the only species that preys on birds.

  c. Eating barn swallows is a rare chance for them.

  d. They can catch birds with their sharp teeth.

SUMMARY

6   Use the words in the box to fill in the blanks.

fast   strategy   freshwater   surface   daily   angle   unusual

South African tigerfish are one of the rare types of _____ fish in the world that feed on birds. Hunting barn swallows is a(n) _____ activity for them. They use an impressive hunting _____ . Tigerfish follow the barn swallows while considering how the light's _____ changes, and then they jump out and catch the birds in mid-air. This is _____ because in most food chains birds hunt fish.

WARM-UP QUESTION • Do you know what the word "abracadabra" means?

The word "abracadabra" is familiar to speakers of many languages. These days, it is mainly used by magicians. They say this "magic" word when they perform a magic trick.

5 But in ancient times, people were more serious about the powers of this word. They believed it could cure fevers and other illnesses.

The first known mention of abracadabra comes from a Roman doctor named Serenus Sammonicus. In the second century A.D., he wrote a poem called *De Medicina*
10 *Praecepta*. The poem tells of an *amulet that sick people wore around their necks. Inside the amulet was a piece of paper with the special word written on it.

The word was written eleven times, but each time it lost its last letter. Finally, in the eleventh row there was only an "A." The amulet was the shape of a triangle. People thought that, together with the word abracadabra, the triangle could remove sickness
15 from the body. The illness would enter the wide top and flow out through the skinny bottom. Once gone, it could not reenter the **narrow** bottom of the triangle.

Descriptions of this amulet are the first recorded evidence of the word abracadabra, but many people theorize that it is even older. Some people think it comes from ancient Hebrew: *Ab*, *Ben*, and *Ruach Cadesh*, which means "Father, Son, and Holy Ghost." Others
20 say it comes from Aramaic (from *Avra kehdabra*, meaning "I will create as I speak"), and still others claim the word is Chaldean. The answer is buried in history and will probably never be known. But one thing is for sure: abracadabra is more than just a word used by magicians when they wave their magic wands.

*amulet: a small object thought to protect its wearer from evil

---

WORD FOCUS

⟷ Antonyms for

narrow

| broad |
| wide |
| extensive |

WORD
CHECK

Choose the correct words for the blanks from the highlighted words in the passage.

1. _____ to come up with a possible explanation for sth uncertain
2. _____ an entertainer who performs illusions
3. _____ sth used to prove a belief
4. _____ to come out of sth quickly and smoothly
5. _____ a line of objects or people arranged side by side

1 What is the passage mainly about?

    a. traditional folk remedies to cure sick people

    b. where the word abracadabra comes from

    c. the favorite magic word of magicians

    d. why the word abracadabra became popular

DETAILS

2 What did people in ancient times believe the word "abracadabra" could do?

_____

3 According to paragraph 3, which best describes the word inside the amulet?

a.	b.	c.	d.
A	A	A-B-R-A-C-A-D-A-B-R-A	A-B-R-A-C-A-D-A-B-R-A
A-B	R-A	A-B-R-A-C-A-D-A-B-R	B-R-A-C-A-D-A-B-R-A
A-B-R	B-R-A	A-B-R-A-C-A-D-A-B	R-A-C-A-D-A-B-R-A
A-B-R-A	A-B-R-A	A-B-R-A-C-A-D-A	A-C-A-D-A-B-R-A
A-B-R-A-C	D-A-B-R-A	A-B-R-A-C-A-D	C-A-D-A-B-R-A
A-B-R-A-C-A	A-D-A-B-R-A	A-B-R-A-C-A	A-D-A-B-R-A
A-B-R-A-C-A-D	C-A-D-A-B-R-A	A-B-R-A-C	D-A-B-R-A
A-B-R-A-C-A-D-A	A-C-A-D-A-B-R-A	A-B-R-A	A-B-R-A
A-B-R-A-C-A-D-A-B	R-A-C-A-D-A-B-R-A	A-B-R	B-R-A
A-B-R-A-C-A-D-A-B-R	B-R-A-C-A-D-A-B-R-A	A-B	R-A
A-B-R-A-C-A-D-A-B-R-A	A-B-R-A-C-A-D-A-B-R-A	A	A

4 Which of the following is NOT true according to the passage?

    a. In the past, some people wore an amulet when they were sick.

    b. The first recorded mention of the word abracadabra was in a poem.

    c. There are several possible meanings of the word abracadabra.

    d. The exact origin of the word abracadabra has been recently revealed.

SUMMARY

5 Match each topic to the correct paragraph in the passage.

    (1) Paragraph 1 •   • ⓐ uses of the word abracadabra through time

    (2) Paragraph 2 •   • ⓑ theories about the word abracadabra's origin

    (3) Paragraph 3 •   • ⓒ beliefs about the abracadabra amulet

    (4) Paragraph 4 •   • ⓓ first evidence of the word abracadabra

The Royal Institution Christmas Lectures began in Great Britain more than 180 years ago. They are held in London every December during the holiday break, which makes it easier for students to attend them. Although the lectures are scientific and given by experts in their fields, they are so easy to understand that even young students can enjoy them.

The lectures were originally proposed by an English scientist named Michael Faraday in 1825. At that time, Faraday was serving as the director of the laboratory at the Royal Institution. He was interested in educating children who were too poor to attend school regularly. Faraday himself came from a poor family and had a difficult time getting a proper education. Inspired by a lecture given by the scientist Humphry Davy, Faraday dedicated himself to science at an early age. Over time, he made many contributions to the field, and he was honored by the government with an offer of a house and a pension. He refused the offer, but recalling his own experience, he requested one thing: _____(A)_____. Thus, the Christmas Lectures were born.

The Christmas Lectures have inspired many people to consider **careers** in the field of science. The mathematician Marcus du Sautoy, who gave a lecture in 2006, was taken to the Christmas Lectures when he was 12. It was that experience that made him decide to become a scientist.

These days, the Christmas Lectures have become a global event. They have been broadcast in various countries including Korea. They can also be watched online now. Whether you are interested in science or not, why not consider listening to one?

WORD CHECK

Choose the correct words for the blanks from the highlighted words in the passage.

1. _____ regular payments made to sb from governments or companies
2. _____ a place for conducting experiments
3. _____ an educational speech
4. _____ a subject or area of knowledge
5. _____ an act of giving sth in order to improve sth else

1 What is the best title for the passage?

   a. An Educational Experiment for Everyone

   b. Celebrating the Holidays in England

   c. Science Lectures That Inspire People

   d. A Science School for Poor Children

2 Which is NOT mentioned about the Christmas Lectures?

   a. the host organization of the lectures

   b. how long the lectures have been held

   c. how the lectures began

   d. when it received attention globally

3 Which is closest in meaning to recalling?

   a. forgetting   b. remembering   c. expecting   d. removing

4 What is the best expression for blank (A)?

   a. that the government support the testing of his theories

   b. that his children be taught through a science class

   c. that a house and a pension be offered to poor people

   d. that poor children be provided with educational opportunities

5 Which is NOT true about Michael Faraday according to the passage?

   a. He was a member of the Royal Institution.

   b. A lecture from Humphry Davy led him to dedicate his life to science.

   c. He was able to hold public lectures with the pension he received.

   d. A childhood experience inspired him to create the Christmas Lectures.

6 Use the words in the box to fill in the blanks.

understandable	scientific	global	annually	educate	properly	attract

The Royal Institution Christmas Lectures have been held _____ in London for over 180 years. They focus on _____ topics, but are designed to be entertaining and _____ for everyone. They were started in 1825 by Michael Faraday, a scientist who wanted to help _____ poor children. These days, the lectures are used to _____ people to the field of science.

WORD REVIEW TEST

[1~4] Choose the word that is closest in meaning to the underlined word.

1. Enough sleep is essential to stay fit.
    a. satisfying   b. pleasing   c. necessary   d. worthy

2. Though she was tiny, she had a very loud voice.
    a. small   b. lazy   c. thirsty   d. intelligent

3. The star is a great distance from Earth.
    a. view   b. field   c. period   d. length

4. The farmer grabbed the goat before it could escape.
    a. fed   b. surprised   c. caught   d. purchased

[5~7] Connect the matching words in columns A and B.

A	B
5. hide from •	• a. enemies
6. fly through •	• b. the water
7. jump out of •	• c. the air

[8~11] Choose the best word to complete each sentence. (Change the form if needed.)

species   extraordinary   flight   broad   environment   angle

8.   The triangle I drew has a(n) _____ of 90 degrees.

9.   There are several thousand _____ of trees here.

10. I know someone with a(n) _____ talent for playing the guitar.

11. An eagle in _____ can see prey from a mile away.

[12~15] Choose the correct word for each definition.

suddenly   spot   design   closely   actual   opposite

12. very carefully or thoroughly:

13. a thing that is the reverse of something else:

14. real, not estimated or imagined:

15. to see something that one is looking for:

[1~3] Choose the word that is closest in meaning to the underlined word.

1. You should always <u>consider</u> the weather when planning a trip.
   a. get through   b. believe in   c. look around   d. think about

2. We are going to <u>request</u> assistance from other countries.
   a. show off   b. pick up   c. ask for   d. look for

3. The man <u>claimed</u> that he had nothing to do with the terror attack.
   a. proved   b. agreed   c. insisted   d. lied

[4~7] Connect the matching words in columns A and B.

A		B
4. write •		• a. school
5. attend •		• b. fevers
6. cure •		• c. a magic trick
7. perform •		• d. a poem

[8~11] Choose the best word to complete each sentence.

8. The soldiers were standing in three _____ in the playground.
   a. rows   b. mentions   c. shapes   d. bottoms

9. They are developing new medicine for AIDS in the _____.
   a. wand   b. pension   c. experience   d. laboratory

10. The experienced _____ changed a rabbit into a pig.
    a. scientist   b. magician   c. director   d. mathematician

11. Susan is very interested in the _____ of international trade.
    a. offer   b. illness   c. field   d. evidence

[12~15] Choose the correct word for each definition.

recall   dedicate   bury   proper   honor   ancient

12. related to the distant past in history:

13. to treat someone with great respect:

14. to bring back the memory of a past event:

15. to offer all of one's energy, time, etc. to something:

WARM-UP QUESTION • What would you buy if you were given 100 dollars?

Today, people consume to meet not only their physical needs but also their psychological needs. For example, when choosing a new smartphone, many people ignore its features. They simply choose a famous brand. In this case, it is the concept of the brand that they consume, not the product itself. This is known as conceptual
5 consumption.

There are several kinds of conceptual consumption. The first involves expectations —when we purchase something, we have an expectation of its value. In one experiment, *pleasure centers in the brain were more active when people thought they were drinking expensive wine rather than cheap wine. In fact, however, both were the same cheap
10 wine. This shows people's expectations can affect how **pleasurable** their experience of consuming is.

The second type of conceptual consumption involves experiences. People want to possess new and interesting experiences they can show off to others. This kind of experience-seeking explains why some people choose to stay in a hotel made of ice rather
15 than a fancy hotel. They are willing to accept an inferior _____(A)_____ experience to enjoy a superior _____(B)_____ one.

The consumption of memories is the final type. People sometimes value the memory of an experience over the experience itself. For example, a <u>couple</u> that eats an amazing meal at a restaurant may never return for a second meal. This is because they worry that a
20 second visit could ruin the special memory of their first experience. This shows concepts sometimes encourage us to consume less rather than more.

Learning about conceptual consumption can help marketers understand the motivations of
25 modern consumers and easily persuade them to purchase products.

*pleasure center: an area of the brain that generates feeling of pleasure

WORD FOCUS

⊜ Synonyms for

pleasurable

enjoyable
delightful
entertaining
satisfying

WORD CHECK

Choose the correct words for the blanks from the highlighted words in the passage.

1. _____ to have or own sth
2. _____ to damage or break sth beyond repair
3. _____ a feeling about how sth will happen or how sb will act
4. _____ to put on display in order to receive praise
5. _____ a reason for doing sth or acting in a certain way

1 **What is the best title for the passage?**

   a. Fulfilling Our Needs Beyond Material Objects

   b. Ideas: The Greatest Creation of Humanity

   c. New Ways to Become a Smart Consumer

   d. High Price Leading to High Demand

DETAILS

2 **What can be inferred from paragraph 2?**

   a. It costs more to produce expensive wine than a cheap one.

   b. Expensive wine actually tastes worse than cheap one.

   c. People expect expensive wine to be tastier than cheap one.

   d. People consider a cheaper price important when choosing wine.

3 **What is the best pair for blanks (A) and (B)?**

	(A)	(B)
a.	physical	material
b.	conceptual	psychological
c.	physical	conceptual
d.	conceptual	physical

4 **The couple in paragraph 4 will not visit the restaurant again because _____.**

   a. they did not enjoy the meal at the first visit

   b. they want to preserve the good memory about it

   c. their good memory about it faded with time

   d. they prefer a new experience to repeating the old one

5 **How can learning about conceptual consumption help marketers?**

_____

SUMMARY

6 **Use the words in the box to fill in the blanks.**

preserve physical value experience less unusual concept

Conceptual Consumption

Consuming Expectations	Consuming Experiences	Consuming Memories
• anticipating a product's (1)_____ in advance • influences our pleasure of consuming	• seeking out (2)_____ experiences • will accept (3)_____ discomfort for a valuable experience	• valuing the memory more than the (4)_____ itself • will avoid a second experience to (5)_____ the first

The World Bank

During World War II, many countries in Europe suffered great destruction. After the war ended, they needed help to rebuild their cities and to improve their economies. The World Bank was founded in 1944 to help these countries by lending them money.

Today the European economy is strong, but the World Bank continues to work. It now
5 lends money to developing countries, providing them with low-interest or interest-free loans. With these loans, a developing country can restructure and improve its economy. This is helpful because, when rich governments give loans, they usually insist on very high interest rates. It also gives poor countries more time to pay the money back, from 15 to 20 years.

The World Bank also helps developing countries in a more direct way. ■ While some
10 organizations simply give food to poor countries, the World Bank uses education as a more long-term solution. ■ This way, there will be more food for everyone, and farmers will make a better living. ■ As a result, they will have more money to put back into the economy. ■

In addition, the World Bank tries to stop the suffering caused by diseases. To improve general health, developing countries need doctors and nurses. The World Bank helps local
15 governments create opportunities for people to get a medical education. This way, more doctors and nurses can help sick people.

The organization does, however, face some criticism for the projects it chooses to support. In 1981, for example, the development program it funded in Brazil led to an increase in rainforest destruction. Also, it allows powerful countries to dominate its
20 decision-making process, often ignoring voices from the nations most directly affected by its actions.

1 According to the passage, the World Bank was founded in 1944

   ⓐ to control European banks

   ⓑ to financially support soldiers

   ⓒ to make money from European countries

   ⓓ to help European countries improve their economies

2 Look at the four squares [■] that indicate where the following sentence could be added to the passage.

It helps farmers learn new farming techniques so that they can grow more food.

Where would the sentence best fit?

3 According to paragraph 4, the World Bank helps developing countries by

   ⓐ sending doctors and nurses

   ⓑ promoting medical education

   ⓒ supporting free medical service

   ⓓ helping sick people make a good living

4 The word dominate in the passage is closest in meaning to

   ⓐ control   ⓑ approve   ⓒ interrupt   ⓓ promote

5 All of the following are mentioned in the passage as the work of the World Bank EXCEPT

   ⓐ providing low-interest loans

   ⓑ teaching new farming techniques

   ⓒ helping to improve general health

   ⓓ bringing clean water and electricity

6   Directions   Look at the sentence in bold. It is the first sentence of a short summary of the passage. Choose THREE answers to complete the summary. Wrong answer choices use minor ideas from the passage or use information that is not in the passage.

The World Bank was founded in 1944.

   ⓐ It helps doctors and nurses to be successful.

   ⓑ It lends money to poor countries to improve their economies.

   ⓒ It promotes education as a long-term solution to relieve poverty.

   ⓓ The majority of its efforts deal with giving food to poor countries.

   ⓔ It causes countries like Brazil to depend on wealthy organizations.

   ⓕ Despite its intentions, it is met with criticism for aiding controversial actions.

WORD REVIEW TEST

[1~4] Choose the word that is closest in meaning to the underlined word.

1. Some people want to <u>possess</u> more than they need.
    a. own   b. lend   c. accept   d. involve

2. This organization was <u>founded</u> 50 years ago.
    a. discovered   b. disassembled   c. improved   d. established

3. We cannot measure the <u>value</u> of learning.
    a. worth   b. concept   c. memory   d. feature

4. Tickets for the festival can be <u>purchased</u> online.
    a. bought   b. borrowed   c. funded   d. encouraged

[5~7] Connect the matching words in columns A and B.

A		B
5. face •		• a. the economy
6. improve •		• b. money
7. lend •		• c. criticism

[8~11] Choose the best word to complete each sentence. (Change the form if needed.)

expectation   persuade   destruction   nation   meet   ignore

8. Jeff _____ my advice and quit his job last week.

9. I didn't want to join the club, but Amy _____ me.

10. The floods caused great _____ to the town.

11. Their _____ for his success were very high.

[12~15] Choose the correct word for each definition.

consume   direct   interest   inferior   rebuild   loan

12. not as good as something else or less important in value:

13. to use goods, services etc.:

14. to make something again after it has been destroyed:

15. a charge that you have to pay in return for borrowing money:

READING EXPERT

A 5-LEVEL READING COURSE for EFL Readers

1

NE_Neungyule

Answers & Explanations

READING EXPERT

A 5-LEVEL READING COURSE for EFL Readers

1

Answers & Explanations

Reading 용어 및 지시문

Ⅰ. 글의 구조와 관련된 용어

- **passage**(지문): 한 주제를 다룬 하나의 짧은 글을 말한다. 여러 개의 단락이 모여 한 지문을 구성한다.
- **paragraph**(단락): 글쓴이가 하나의 주제에 대하여 전개해 나가는 서로 연관된 여러 문장의 집합을 말한다. 흔히 들여쓰기로 단락과 단락 사이를 구분한다.
- **main idea**(요지): 글쓴이가 말하고자 하는 바, 즉 중심이 되는 견해로 보통 문장으로 표현된다.
- **topic sentence**(주제문): 글쓴이의 중심적 견해를 담고 있는 문장으로 각 단락에는 topic sentence가 있다.

Ⅱ. 지시문

- **What is the best title for the passage?** (이 글에 가장 알맞은 제목은?)
- **What is the passage mainly about?** (이 글은 주로 무엇에 관한 내용인가?)
- **What is the main idea of the passage?** (이 글의 중심생각[요지]은 무엇인가?)
- **What is the best word [expression] for blank (A)?** (빈칸 (A)에 들어갈 말로 가장 알맞은 것은?)
- **What is the best pair for blanks (A) and (B)?** (빈칸 (A)와 (B)에 들어갈 말을 짝지은 것 중 가장 적절한 것은?)
- **Which is closest in meaning to <u>appreciated</u>?** (<u>appreciated</u>의 의미와 가장 가까운 것은?)
- **What does the underlined part mean?** (밑줄 친 부분이 의미하는 것은?)
- **What can be inferred from the underlined part?** (밑줄 친 부분에서 유추할 수 있는 것은?)
- **Which of the following is NOT mentioned in the passage?** (다음 중 이 글에서 언급되지 않은 것은?)
- **Which of the following is NOT true according to the passage?** (다음 중 본문의 내용과 일치하지 않는 것은?)
- **Write T if the statement is true or F if it's false.** (진술이 참이면 T, 거짓이면 F를 쓰시오.)
- **Where would the following sentence best fit?** (다음 문장이 들어갈 위치로 가장 알맞은 곳은?)
- **Use the words in the box to fill in the blanks.** (상자 안의 단어를 골라 빈칸을 채우시오.)
- **Match each topic to the correct paragraph in the passage.** (각 주제와 본문의 단락을 알맞게 연결하시오.)

UNIT 01.
Teens

WORD CHECK

1. pain   2. shy   3. have a crush on   4. hang out
5. ruin

▶ gentle: kind; doing things thoughtfully and cautiously

정답

1. c   2. d   3. c   4. He or she feels romantic, confused, and in pain all at once.   5. d   6. feelings, pain, gently, romantic, ruining

해석

엘라 선생님께

제게 커다란 문제가 하나 생겼어요! 제 이웃 중에 니콜이라는 이름의 여자아이가 있어요. 그 애와 저는 평생 동안 친구였고 늘 같이 놀러 다녔요. 어제까지만 해도 모든 게 다 괜찮았어요. 방과 후에 집으로 걸어가는 중에 니콜이 저를 사랑한다고 고백했어요! 그 애는 너무 부끄러워서 진작 말을 못 했대요. 하지만 저는 그 애가 제게 그 말을 아예 하지 않았더라면 좋았을 거예요. 저는 그 애가 괜찮은 여자아이라고 생각하고, 그 애와 같이 시간을 보내는 것을 정말 좋아해요. 하지만 엘라 선생님, 저는 그 애를 사랑하진 않아요! 전 사실 학교의 다른 여자아이에게 반해 있거든요. 에이미라는 아이예요. 제가 니콜을 사랑하지 않는다는 것을 어떻게 얘기해야 하죠? 저는 우리가 친구로 남았으면 좋겠어요.

토니 드림

토니에게

저런. 참 곤란한 문제가 생겼군요! 니콜이 학생에게 무척 반해있는 것 같네요. (누군가에게) 푹 빠지면, 낭만적이고 혼란스럽고 고통스러운 감정을 동시에 느끼죠! 당신이 니콜을 사랑하지 않는다는 걸 알면 니콜은 괴로울 거예요. 이 말은 곧 학생이 그녀를 아주 정중하게 대해야 한다는 것입니다. 제 조언은 우정을 깨뜨리고 싶지 않다고 그녀에게 말하라는 겁니다. 둘이 함께한 즐거움에 관해 얘기하고, 학생이 그녀를 얼마나 좋아하는지 그녀가 확실히 알게 하세요. 하지만 낭만적으로 들리지 않게끔 조심해야 합니다. 그녀가 학생의 친구이기를 원하지 여자친구이기를 원하는 게 아니라는 점을 분명히 하세요. 또한 학생이 좋아하는 여학생의 이름을 말하지 않도록 조심하세요. 학생이 그 이름을 말하는 것을 니콜이 들으면 그녀의 마음은 훨씬 더 아플 겁니다. 행운을 빌어요, 토니!

엘라 선생님이

구문 해설

5행 She said she was **too** shy **to tell** me before.
▶ too ~ to-v: 너무 ~하여 …할 수 없다

5행 But **I wish** she **had** never **told** me.
▶ I wish + 가정법 과거완료(주어 + had p.p.): (과거에) ~였더라면 좋을 텐데

12행 What a difficult problem you have!

▶ What으로 시작하는 감탄문의 어순은 「What + a(n) + 형용사 + 명사 + 주어 + 동사」

17행 But be very careful **not to sound** romantic.
▶ to부정사의 부정은 to부정사 앞에 not을 붙여 나타냄

18행 Make **it** clear **that** you want her to be your friend, not your girlfriend.
▶ it은 가목적어, that 이하가 진목적어

WORD FOCUS   stage

the early stages 초기 / a critical stage 중대한 시기 / reach a stage 단계에 들어가다[이르다] / go through a stage 시기를 겪다, 단계를 거치다

WORD CHECK

1. toddler   2. connection   3. excuse   4. absorb
5. judgment

▶ strengthen: to cause sth to become stronger

정답

1. c   2. b   3. Because the brain cells and nerve connections that are used the most become stronger, while those that are used the least die off.   4. d   5. a
6. development, chooses, often, rarely, good

해석

당신은 당신의 뇌가 일생 동안 변한다는 것을 알고 있었는가? 당신이 걸음마를 시작한 아이였을 때, 뇌는 당신 주위의 모든 것을 흡수하는 스펀지 같았다. 그 당시에, 당신의 부모는 당신의 뇌 발달을 이끌고 형성하도록 도왔다. 당신의 십 대 시절은 또 다른 중요한 (발달) 단계이다. 그리고 이 시기에 당신은 뇌가 변하는 방식에 영향을 미칠 기회를 가진다.

과학자들은 13세에서 25세 사이에 당신의 뇌가 선택의 과정을 거친다고 말한다. 가장 많이 쓰이는 뇌세포와 신경 연결은 더 강화되는 반면, 가장 적게 쓰이는 것들은 소멸한다. 이것이 바로 이 시기에 건전한 활동에 참여하는 것이 중요한 이유이다. 예를 들어, 많은 시간을 바이올린을 연습하는 데 할애하는 것은 음악 학습에 관련된 뇌 연결을 강화한다. 하지만 TV를 많이 보면, 뇌는 그것에 익숙해질 것이다. 또한, 판단을 내리는 데 쓰이는 뇌 부위가 아직 완전하게 발달하지 않았다. 이것은 십 대가 보통 감정에 기초하여 행동하고, 심지어 그들에게 좋지 않은 것인데도, 친구들이 하는 것을 따라 한다는 것을 의미한다. 이는 왜 일부 십 대들이 담배를 피우고 술을 마시는지를 설명하는 데 도움이 될지도 모른다. 비록 그것이 그러한 행동들에 대한 변명이 될 수는 없지만 말이다.

당신이 뇌에서 일어나고 있는 변화에 대해 안다면 자신이 잘못된 결정을 내리는 것을 막을 수 있다. 당신이 십 대에 하는 일이 당신의 여생에 영향을 미칠 수도 있다는 것을 잊지 마라. 행동하기 전에 항상 신중히 생각하고 건전한 선택을 하도록 최선을 다하라!

2행 ..., it was like a <u>sponge</u> [that absorbed everything around you].

6행 And this time you have <u>the opportunity</u> **to affect** [*how* it changes].

▶ to affect는 the opportunity를 수식하는 형용사적 용법의 to부정사

▶ how가 이끄는 절은 affect의 목적어 역할

9행 <u>The brain cells and nerve connections</u> [that are used
S
the most] <u>become</u> stronger, **while** *those* [that are
V   S'
used the least] <u>die off</u>.
V'

▶ while: ~인 반면

▶ those는 앞에 나온 명사구 The brain cells and nerve connections를 대신함

11행 For example, **spending** a lot of time **practicing** the
S
violin <u>strengthens</u> <u>the brain connections</u> [involved
V   O
in learning music].

▶ spend + 시간 + v-ing: ~하면서 시간을 보내다

19행 You can **stop** yourself **from making** bad decisions if
you know about <u>the changes</u> [that are happening in
your brain].

▶ stop + 목적어 + from v-ing: ~이 …하는 것을 막다

20행 Don't forget that **what** <u>you do</u> as a teenager <u>can</u>
S'   V'
<u>affect</u> the rest of your life.

▶ what은 선행사를 포함하는 관계대명사로, what이 이끄는 절이 that절 안에서 주어 역할을 함

UNIT 02.
People

READING 1   p. 12~13

WORD FOCUS   issue

a big issue 큰 쟁점, 커다란 문제 / a major issue 큰 화제, 주요 쟁점 / resolve an issue 문제를 해결하다 / raise an issue 문제를 제기하다

WORD CHECK

1. explore   2. damaging   3. invention
4. fascination   5. underwater

▶ society: an organization for people who have a special interest

1. d   2. b   3. It refers to the damaging effects of human activity on ocean environments.   4. d
5. discover, inventors, camera, research, dangers

바다 밑의 세계는 매혹적이다. 고래들과 다채로운 물고기들이 물살을 가르며 평화롭게 헤엄치는 것을 보는 것은 놀라운 일이다. 자크 이브 쿠스토는 우리가 이런 환경과 그 경이들을 탐험하는 것을 가능하게 해 준 사람 중 하나였다. 그는 1910년 프랑스에서 태어났으며 수영과 수중 세계를 관찰하는 데 평생 매료되었다.

1943년에 쿠스토는 프랑스인 공학자 에밀 가냥의 도움으로 최초의 잠수용 호흡기를 만들었다. 이 기기는 사람들이 공기를 위해 위로 올라올 필요 없이, 오랫동안 수중에 머무르는 것을 가능하게 해 주었다. 현대의 스쿠버 다이빙은 이 발명품으로부터 발전했다. 쿠스토는 또한 심해에서 사용될 수 있는 카메라를 만들어, 그것을 그의 첫 번째 해양 다큐멘터리를 촬영하는 데 사용했다.

이 외에도 쿠스토는 바다 아래 가라앉은 로마 제국의 배를 잠수부 및 과학자들과 함께 탐험했는데, 그것은 최초의 수중 고고학 연구였다. 그는 그가 바다에 대해 알게 된 모든 것을 다른 이들과 공유하고 싶어 책을 집필하기 시작했고 〈자크 쿠스토의 해저 세계〉라는 텔레비전 시리즈를 촬영했다. 그 프로그램은 1968년에 시작되어 아홉 시즌 동안 계속되었다. 그것은 바닷속 세계의 아름다움을 수백만 사람들의 가정으로 가져다주었다.

말년에, 자크 이브 쿠스토는 인간의 활동이 해양 환경에 미치는 해로운 영향들에 관해 우려하기 시작했다. 1973년에 그는 이 중요한 사안에 대해 사람들의 관심을 끌고자 쿠스토 협회를 설립했다. 오늘날, 이 협회에는 세계 해양을 보호하는 데 줄곧 힘쓰고 있는 300,000명 이상의 회원이 있다.

2행 **It** is amazing **to see** whales and colorful fish swim peacefully through the water.

▶ It은 가주어, to see 이하가 진주어

4행 ... was one of <u>the people</u> [who made **it** possible *for us*
to explore this environment and its wonders].

▶ it은 가목적어, to explore 이하가 진목적어이며, for us는 to explore의 의미상의 주어

13행 Cousteau also created <u>a camera</u> [that could be used deep underwater], and he used it **to film** his first sea documentaries.

▶ to film은 목적을 나타내는 부사적 용법의 to부정사

15행 In addition, Cousteau explored a sunken Roman ship beneath the ocean with divers and scientists, **which** was ....

▶ which는 앞 절을 대신하는 계속적 용법의 관계대명사

16행 He wanted to share everything [(that) he learned about the sea with others], ... and filmed a television series [called *The Undersea World of Jacques Cousteau*].

▶ he 앞에 everything을 선행사로 하는 목적격 관계대명사 that이 생략됨

READING 2   p. 14~15

WORD FOCUS   found

establish 설립하다 / organize 조직하다, 창립하다 / set up 건립하다

WORD CHECK

1. requirement   2. balanced   3. immigrant
4. labor   5. settlement house

▶ independent: not needing outside help

정답

1. a   2. b   3. It allowed them to share their knowledge and skills with the local people.   4. (1) T (2) F   5. c   6. (1) ⓑ (2) ⓓ (3) ⓒ (4) ⓐ

해석

　역사를 통틀어서, 많은 용감한 사람들이 인권을 위해 싸워왔다. 제인 애덤스는 이러한 사람들 중 한 명이었다. 애덤스는 1860년에 태어났다. 그녀는 새로운 세대인 교육 받은 독립적 미국 여성들의 일부였다. 1888년, 그녀는 친구와 함께 영국 런던으로 여행을 갔다. 그들은 토인비 홀을 방문했는데, 그곳은 '사회 복지관'이라고 불리는 새로운 종류의 자선 단체였다. 그것은 가난한 동네에 사는 사람들을 돕기 위해 빈곤 지역에 세워졌다. 그 두 여성은 그 아이디어를 미국으로 가져오기로 결정했다.

　이듬해, 애덤스와 그녀의 친구는 미국 최초의 사회 복지관인 헐 하우스를 설립했다. 그것은 시카고의 가난한 지역에 위치해 있었고 교육을 받은 여성들이 자신의 지식과 기술을 그 지역의 사람들과 공유할 수 있도록 했다. 중요한 서비스도 제공되었는데, 이민자들을 위한 영어 수업과 직업 훈련을 포함했다. 헐 하우스는 또한 주민 센터, 체육관, 그리고 미술관도 제공했다.

　다음으로, 애덤스는 아동 노동을 끝내는 데에 집중하기 시작했다. 그 당시에는, 많은 어린이들이 안전하지 않은 환경의 공장에서 일하고 있었다. 1902년, 그녀는 아동 노동의 부정적 영향에 대해 사람들을 교육하는 단체를 공동 설립했다. 애덤스는 균형 잡힌 교육이 아이들을 더 나은 시민으로 만들 것이라 믿었다. 그래서 헐 하우스는 그들에게 광범위한 수업들을 제공했다. 머지않아, 아동 교육은 전국적으로 필수 조건이 되었다.

　도움이 필요한 사람들을 돕는 것 외에, 애덤스는 그녀의 삶을 세계 평화에도 바쳤다. 제1차 세계 대전이 시작된 후에, 애덤스는 기사를 작성하고 연설을 함으로써 세계의 평화를 위해 일하기 시작했다. 그녀의 일생에 걸

친 노력의 결과로, 1931년에 그녀는 노벨 평화상을 수상한 최초의 미국 여성이 되었다.

구문 해설

4행 They visited Toynbee Hall, **which** was a new kind of charity [called a "settlement house."]

▶ which는 Toynbee Hall을 선행사로 하는 계속적 용법의 관계대명사 (= and it)

8행 It was located in a poor part of Chicago and **allowed** educated women **to** *share* their knowledge and skills *with* the local people.

▶ allow + 목적어 + to-v: ~이 …하도록 해 주다
▶ share A with B: A를 B와 나누다[공유하다]

13행 In 1902, she co-founded a group [**that** educated people about the negative effects of child labor].

▶ that은 a group을 선행사로 하는 주격 관계대명사

22행 ..., she became the first American woman **to win** the Nobel Peace Prize in 1931.

▶ to win은 the first American woman을 수식하는 형용사적 용법의 to부정사

WORD REVIEW TEST

UNIT 01   p. 16

1. b   2. c   3. d   4. b   5. b   6. c   7. a   8. shy
9. hang out   10. strengthen   11. absorb
12. development   13. careful   14. confused
15. nerve

UNIT 02   p. 17

1. d   2. c   3. c   4. c   5. d   6. a   7. b   8. a
9. d   10. a   11. d   12. device   13. effect
14. neighborhood   15. charity

UNIT 03.
Health

READING 1 p. 18~19

WORD CHECK

1. perishable 2. mild 3. symptom 4. poultry
5. utensil
▶ severe: very serious, intense, or extreme

정답

1. c 2. d 3. d 4. Because food poisoning can sometimes lead to severe dehydration for them.
5. c 6. contaminated, vomiting, hands, perishable, temperature

해석

식중독은 상하거나 오염된 음식을 먹어서 생기는 질병의 한 종류입니다. 식중독은 사람들을 심하게 아프게 할 수 있습니다. 따라서, 그것의 증상과 그것을 예방하기 위해 우리가 무엇을 할 수 있는지 아는 것이 중요합니다.

Q: 식중독의 원인은 무엇입니까?
A: 식중독은 날음식이나 오염된 물에 있는 박테리아나 바이러스에 의해 발생합니다. 식중독을 일으키는 흔한 박테리아 집단 중 하나는 살모넬라균입니다. 살모넬라균은 날고기나 덜 익은 고기, 가금류, 우유, 그리고 달걀에서 발견될 수 있습니다. 또 다른 것은 비브리오 패혈균이라고 불리는 박테리아의 한 종류입니다. 그것은 바닷물에 존재하고 날 해산물에 의해 옮겨집니다. 마지막으로, 노로바이러스는 씻지 않은 농작물과 오염된 조개류에서 발견될 수 있습니다. 여러분은 감염자와의 접촉을 통해서도 노로바이러스에 감염될 수 있습니다. 식중독을 일으키는 대부분의 박테리아가 여름에 흔하지만, 노로바이러스는 겨울에 더 흔합니다.

Q: 식중독의 증상은 무엇입니까?
A: 식중독의 흔한 증상은 메스꺼움, 설사, 그리고 구토를 포함합니다. 다른 증상은 복통, 흐린 시야, 그리고 현기증을 포함합니다. 대부분의 경우, 식중독은 가볍게 지나갑니다. 그러나, 어린이들이나 노인들은 비교적 몸이 약하여 때때로 심한 탈수로 이어질 수 있습니다. 따라서, 증상들이 나타나면 그들은 병원에 가야 할 필요가 있을 수도 있습니다.

Q: 식중독은 어떻게 예방될 수 있습니까?
A: 첫째, 음식을 다루기 전후에 따뜻한 비눗물로 손을 씻고 모든 식기를 깨끗이 유지하세요. 또한, 여러분은 부패하기 쉬운 음식은 구매한 지 두 시간 이내에 항상 냉장 또는 냉동시켜야 합니다. 조리할 때에는, 교차 오염을 방지하기 위해서 날음식은 바로 먹을 수 있는 음식(즉석식품)과는 언제나 분리해야 합니다. 마지막으로, 반드시 여러분의 음식이 안전한 온도에 도달할 때까지 요리하세요.

구문 해설

[3행] Therefore, **it** is important **to know** about its symptoms and [*what* we can do to prevent it].
▶ it은 가주어, to know 이하가 진주어
▶ what이 이끄는 절은 전치사 about의 목적어로 쓰인 간접의문문으로, its symptoms와 병렬 관계

[8행] One common group of bacteria [**that** causes food poisoning] is Salmonella.
▶ that은 One common group of bacteria를 선행사로 하는 주격 관계대명사

[17행] However, it can sometimes lead to severe dehydration for children and the elderly, **who** are relatively weak.
▶ who는 계속적 용법의 주격 관계대명사 (= and they)

[23행] **When cooking**, always *keep* raw foods *separate* from ready-to-eat foods **to prevent** cross contamination.
▶ When cooking은 접속사가 생략되지 않은 분사구문 (= When you cook)
▶ keep + 목적어 + 형용사: ~을 …한 상태로 유지하다
▶ to prevent는 목적을 나타내는 부사적 용법의 to부정사

READING 2 p. 20~21

WORD FOCUS influence

a strong influence 강력한 영향(력) / a negative influence 부정적인 영향 / political influence 정치적 영향(력) / have influence on ~에 영향을 미치다

WORD CHECK

1. hometown 2. mysterious 3. settle
4. overweight 5. found
▶ fatty: being high in fat

정답

1. d 2. Nicola Rosato called it Roseto after his hometown. 3. ⓒ 4. c 5. d 6. (1) ⓒ (2) ⓐ (3) ⓓ (4) ⓑ

해석

19세기 후반, 이탈리아의 가난한 마을인 로세토 발포르토레의 주민 거의 모두가 미국의 한 소도시로 이주했다. 이 소도시는 니콜라 로사토에 의해 1887년 펜실베이니아주에 만들어졌는데, 그는 그곳을 자기 고향의 이름을 따서 로세토라고 불렀다. 그곳에 정착한 이탈리아 이민자들은 더 나은 삶을 찾고 있었다.
1960년대에 스튜어트 울프라는 이름의 의사가 로세토에서 매우 놀라운 것을 발견했다. 그곳에 거주하는 모든 사람을 연구한 끝에, 그는 그들이

나라의 여타 지역 사람들보다 일반적으로 훨씬 더 건강하다는 것을 알게 되었다. 그 도시에서 심장병으로 사망하는 사람의 수가 국가 평균의 절반이었다. 사실상, 55세 미만인 사람 중에 심장 마비로 사망한 사람은 거의 없었다. 그리고 다른 원인으로 인한 사망률도 국가 평균보다 35% 낮았다. 많은 사람이 단순히 고령으로 사망했다.

그렇다면, 로세토 사람들의 비결은 무엇이었을까? 울프의 결과에 따르면 그것은 확실히 습관 때문은 아니었다. 그들은 기름진 음식을 많이 먹었고, 많은 사람이 고도의 비만이었다. <u>게다가, 그들은 몸에 매우 무리가 가는 일을 장시간 했다.</u> 그들이 왜 그렇게 건강한지에 대한 명확한 의학적 설명이 없었다. 그래서 연구자들은 로세토 사람들의 아주 좋은 건강 상태는 그 도시 자체로부터 비롯된 것이라고 결론 내렸다. 로세토는 긴밀히 연결된 가족 공동체였다. 대부분의 아이, 부모, 그리고 조부모가 한 지붕 아래에서 살았고, 모든 사람이 교회, 축제, 그리고 사회 활동에 참여했다.

과학자들은 가족과 사회생활이 건강에 미치는 이 신비한 영향을 '로세토 효과(Roseto Effect)'라고 부른다. 그것은 다른 사람들과 긴밀한 관계를 유지하는 것이 사람들로 하여금 건강에 좋지 않은 일상 스트레스를 줄이도록 도울 수 있음을 보여 준다.

구문 해설

[1행] ..., almost all of the people [from the poor Italian
village of Roseto Valfortore] moved to a town in the
United States.

[2행] This town was founded in the state of Pennsylvania
in 1887 by Nicola Rosato, **who** called it Roseto after
his hometown.
▶ who는 계속적 용법의 주격 관계대명사 (= and he)

[5행] ..., a doctor [named Stewart Wolf] discovered
something very **surprising** in Roseto.
▶ -thing으로 끝나는 (대)명사는 형용사가 뒤에서 수식

[20행] It shows {that *having* close connections with others
can **help** people **reduce** the everyday stresses [that
are bad for one's health]}.
▶ 첫 번째 that은 접속사, 두 번째 that은 주격 관계대명사
▶ that이 이끄는 명사절 안에서 동명사구인 having ... others
가 주어로 쓰임
▶ help + 목적어 + (to)-v: ~이 …하도록 돕다

UNIT 04.
Food

READING 1   p. 22~23

WORD FOCUS ordinary

normal 보통의 / typical 전형적인 / usual 평소의, 보통의

WORD CHECK

1. texture   2. pregnant   3. ratio   4. raw
5. ingredient
▶ potential: ability or quality that may grow or become
successful in the future

정답

1. d   2. They build it layer by layer.   3. b   4. (1) T
(2) F   5. c   6. nutrients, ratio, Saves, customized,
health

해석

당신은 부엌으로 걸어 들어가서 단순히 화면을 건드림으로써 당신이 원하는 어떤 음식이든 만들어내는 것을 상상할 수 있는가? 3D 인쇄는 곧 이것을 가능하게 할지도 모른다. 3D 프린터는 층층이 쌓아서 거의 모든 종류의 물건을 생산할 수 있다. 현재 과학자들은 초콜릿이나 심지어는 고기 같은 음식들을 '인쇄'하기 위해서 그것들을 사용하고 있다. 그렇다면 그것은 어떻게 작동할까?

3D 음식 인쇄는 사실 아주 간단하다. 우선 당신은 프린터에 원료를 넣는다. 이것들은 모든 음식에 공통적이다. 그것(원료)들은 단백질, 탄수화물, 지방이다. 다음으로 어떤 비율을 사용할지 프린터에 지시한다. 그러고 나서 프린터가 음식을 만들어내는 동안 기다린다. 이런 방식으로, 사람들은 그들의 필요에 따라 음식을 만들 수 있다. 예를 들어, 운동선수는 고단백 파스타를 인쇄할 수 있을 것이다. 혹은 임신한 여성은 비타민이 추가로 들어간 빵을 인쇄할 수 있을 것이다. 그뿐만 아니라, 알레르기가 있는 사람은 특정 성분을 빼도록 프린터에 지시할 수 있을 것이다.

3D 음식 인쇄는 많은 이점을 제공하는 것 같다. 첫 번째로, 음식을 인쇄하는 것은 시간을 절약할 수 있다. 음식을 요리하는 대신, 사람들은 다른 일을 하면서 그것을 인쇄할 수 있다. 두 번째로, 인쇄된 음식은 일반적인 음식보다 맛이 더 좋을 수 있다. 그것은 사람들이 개개인에 맞춘 맛으로 음식을 인쇄할 수 있기 때문이다. 세 번째로, 그것은 음식 디자인에 있어 흥미진진한 가능성을 열어 줄 것 같다. 다양한 질감과 모양을 낼 수 있기 때문에, 당신이 원하는 어떤 디자인도 가능하다. 마지막으로, 그것은 우리의 건강을 향상시킬 수 있다. 사람들이 가공식품의 건강하지 않은 성분들을 더 건강한 선택들로 쉽게 대체할 수 있게 함으로써, 그것은 더욱 영양가 있는 식단을 제공하도록 도와줄 수 있는 잠재력을 가지고 있다. 이렇게 많은 장점으로, 3D 인쇄는 음식 산업의 미래를 완전히 바꿀지도 모른다.

구문 해설

[1행] Can you imagine
- **walking** into your kitchen
- and
- **producing** any food ... *by touching* a screen?
  - ▶ walking과 producing은 imagine의 목적어로 쓰인 동명사
  - ▶ by v-ing: ~함으로써

[9행] Next you tell the printer what ratio to use.
S　V　IO　　DO

[16행] Instead of cooking food, people could print it **while doing** other things.
- ▶ while doing 이하는 접속사가 생략되지 않은 분사구문

[20행] By **allowing** people **to** easily *replace* the unhealthy ingredients in processed foods *with* healthier options, ...
- ▶ allow + 목적어 + to-v: ~이 …하도록 해 주다
- ▶ replace A with B: A를 B로 대체하다

READING 2　　　　　　　　　p. 24~25

WORD FOCUS　healthy

healthy eating 건강한 식사[식생활] / a healthy lifestyle 건강한 생활 방식 / a healthy appetite 건강한 식성 / physically healthy 육체적으로 건강한

WORD CHECK

1. advantage　2. source　3. diet　4. suffer from
5. suitable
▶ climate: the general weather of an area

정답

1. d　2. b　3. b　4. It is good for people with high levels of cholesterol.　5. d　6. diet, vegetables, advantages, healthy

해석

　　모든 나라의 대표 음식들과 마찬가지로, 그리스 고유의 음식은 (지리적) 위치의 결과이다. 그리스는 삼면이 바다로 둘러싸여 있어 언제나 싱싱한 생선을 구할 수 있다. 따뜻하고 건조한 기후는 과일과 채소를 재배하는 데 적당하다. 포도는 햇빛 아래에서 쉽게 자랄 수 있다. 그리고 많은 올리브 나무는 올리브 열매의 원천이다. 이 모든 자연적 요인들이 그리스 사람들에게 건강에 매우 좋은 식단을 제공해 준다.

　　그리스 요리는 많은 채소를 사용하는데, 이것들은 비타민의 중요 공급원이다. 따라서 그리스 음식을 먹는 사람들이 건강할 가능성이 높다는 사실은 놀라운 일이 아니다. 요즈음 과학자들은 특정 채소들이 실제로 심각한 질병을 퇴치해 줄 수 있다는 사실을 발견하고 있다. 예를 들어, 그리스 요리에 흔히 사용되는 토마토는 특정 종류의 암을 예방하는 데 도움이 된다.

　　전통적인 그리스 음식은 또 하나의 주요 사망 원인인 심장병도 예방한다. 많은 그리스 음식에 생선을 사용하는데, 이는 콜레스테롤 수치가 높은 사람들에게 좋다. 일부 그리스 음식은 기름기가 아주 많음에도 불구하고 심장병을 앓는 그리스인은 극히 드물다. 이에 대해서는 두 가지 이유가 있는 것 같다. 첫째, 그리스 사람들은 식사와 함께 종종 적포도주를 조금 마시는데 과학자들은 이것이 심장병을 예방하는 데 효능이 있다고 본다. 둘째, 거의 모든 그리스 음식은 올리브유를 사용해 만들어진다. 이것은 건강에 가장 좋은 형태의 기름 중 하나로, 비타민이 풍부하고 콜레스테롤은 없다.

　　현대 의학은 건강한 식습관에 관한 훌륭한 제안들을 한다. 하지만 수백 년 동안 그리스인들은 질병을 퇴치해 주는 몸에 좋은 음식을 계속 먹어 왔다. 우리가 모두 그리스로 이사를 할 수는 없지만, 그리스식으로 먹는 것은 우리 모두에게 이익이 될 수 있을 것이다.

구문 해설

[10행] Therefore, **it** is not surprising **that** people [who eat Greek food] *are likely to be* healthy.
- ▶ it은 가주어, that 이하는 진주어
- ▶ be likely to-v: ~일 것 같다, ~할 가능성이 있다

[16행] ..., **very few** Greeks suffer from heart disease.
- ▶ very few: 극히 드문 (부정의 의미)

[16행] **There seem to be** two reasons for this.
- ▶ there seem to be: ~이 있는 것 같다

[19행] This is **one of the healthiest types** of oil, full of vitamins and with no cholesterol.
- ▶ one of the + 최상급 + 복수명사: 가장 ~한 …중 하나

WORD REVIEW TEST

UNIT 03　　　　　　　　　p. 26

1. b　2. d　3. c　4. b　5. c　6. a　7. b
8. settled　9. refrigerate　10. Mild　11. medical
12. separate　13. conclude　14. average
15. blurry

UNIT 04　　　　　　　　　p. 27

1. c　2. a　3. d　4. b　5. b　6. c　7. a　8. factor
9. layers　10. raw　11. allergy　12. ordinary
13. leave out　14. climate　15. athlete

UNIT 05.
Society

READING 1   p. 28~29

WORD FOCUS profit

turn a profit 이익을 내다 / maximize profits 이익을 극대화하다 / a huge profit 막대한 수익[이익] / a handsome profit 상당한 수익[이익]

WORD CHECK

1. nonprofit   2. invest   3. consumer   4. remote
5. donate

▶ expand: to grow in size, number or variety

정답

1. b   2. d   3. It assists with medical research that may lead to cures for serious diseases.   4. d   5. connects, donates, profits, society

해석

요즘에는 많은 기업이 기업의 사회적 책임(CSR)에 관심을 보인다. CSR에는 지역 사회에 대한 투자나 환경 보호 같은 것들이 포함된다. 그러한 활동은 기업과 기업의 제품 모두의 평판을 높여 준다. 결과적으로 이것은 재정 수익의 증가로 이어질 수 있다.

기업이 CSR을 실천할 수 있는 여러 가지 방법이 있다. 예를 들어, IBM은 사람들이 세계 공동체 전산망에 참여하는 것을 돕고 있다. 그들은 개인용 컴퓨터를 위한 소규모 프로그램을 만들었다. 컴퓨터가 사용되지 않을 때마다, 그 프로그램이 컴퓨터의 처리 능력을 세계 공동체 전산망의 슈퍼컴퓨터로 기부한다. 이 슈퍼컴퓨터는 심각한 질병에 대한 치료법 개발로 이어질 수 있는 의학 연구를 돕는다.

다음으로 스타벅스가 있다. 이 기업은 커피를 재배하는 지역 사회 거주민의 삶을 개선하기 위해 비영리 단체와 함께 일한다. 예를 들어, 과테말라에서 스타벅스는 세이브더칠드런과 협력해 외딴 마을에 교육 프로그램을 제공한다.

마지막으로, 어떤 기업들은 CSR을 실천하기 위해 특별히 만들어진다. 블레이크 마이코스키가 설립한 탐스 슈즈가 한 예이다. 마이코스키는 2006년에 아르헨티나 전역을 여행하면서 많은 아이들이 신발이 없는 것을 보았다. 현재, 탐스 슈즈는 전 세계적으로 신발을 판매한다. 그들이 판매하는 각각의 켤레에 대해, 개발 도상국의 아이에게 한 켤레씩 기부한다. 그들은 지금까지 전 세계적으로 삼천오백만 켤레 이상의 신발을 기부해 왔다.

CSR은 기업들이 이윤을 내는 것뿐만이 아니라 사회를 개선하기 위해서도 일하고 있음을 소비자들에게 보여주도록 돕는다. 이것은 소비자들이 이러한 기업이 만든 제품을 고를 가능성을 높여 준다. 이런 까닭에 CSR은 앞으로도 확대될 것 같다.

구문 해설

[6행] In turn, **this** can lead to increased financial returns.
▶ this가 가리키는 것은 앞 문장의 내용, 즉 '기업과 기업의 제품 모두의 평판을 높여주는 것'임

[13행] This business works together with nonprofit organizations **to improve** the lives of people {*living* in communities [that grow coffee]}.
▶ to improve는 목적을 나타내는 부사적 용법의 to부정사
▶ living 이하는 people을 수식하는 현재분사구
▶ that은 주격 관계대명사

[17행] TOMS Shoes, [founded by Blake Mycoskie], is one example.
   S   V

[22행] ... they are **not only** making profits **but** (**also**) working to improve society.
▶ not only A but (also) B: A뿐만 아니라 B도

[23행] This makes the consumers **more likely to choose** products [made by these companies].
▶ more likely to-v: 더 ~할 것 같은

READING 2   TOEFL   p. 30~31

정답

1. c   2. d   3. the third square   4. c   5. a
6. b, d, e

해석

북크로싱

'누군가를 사랑한다면 그들을 자유롭게 해 줘라.'라는 옛 속담이 있다. 론 혼베이커는 이 말이 책에도 적용된다고 생각한 사람이었다. 그는 자신이 아주 좋아하는 책들이 책장에서 먼지가 쌓여가는 모습을 보고 싶지 않았다. 그는 그것들을 다른 사람들과 공유하는 것을 꿈꿨다. 그의 목표는 사람들이 그들의 책을 공짜로 나눠 볼 수 있도록 '전 세계를 도서관으로 만드는' 것이었다.

혼베이커는 사람들에게 다른 사람들이 찾을 수 있도록 그들의 책을 공공장소에 두라고 권하고 싶었다. 그는 이것이 재미있는 일이 되도록 www.bookcrossing.com이라는 웹 사이트를 만들었다. 이 웹 사이트를 이용하여 사람들은 책을 다른 사람들과 공유함으로써 계속해서 책을 즐길 수 있다. 그리하여 책을 다 읽었어도 독서의 즐거움은 끝나지 않는다.

그 과정은 '3R'이라 불리는 읽고(Read), 등록하고(Register), 내놓는(Release) 간단한 구조로 되어 있다. 우선, 누군가가 어떤 책을 읽는다. 그 다음에 그 사람은 그 책을 웹 사이트에 등록한다. 그러면 그 책은 ID 번호를 부여받는데, 그 번호는 책의 표지 안쪽에 기록된다. 마지막으로, 그 사람은 책을 커피숍이나 기차역 같은 공공장소에 둠으로써 그 책을 내놓는다. 일단 누군가가 그 책을 발견하면 그 사람은 기대감을 안고 웹 사이트에 방

문해서 '그 책을 찾았다'고 말할 것이다. 이런 식으로, 그 책의 원래 주인은 자신의 책이 발견되었다는 것을 알 수 있게 된다. 그런 다음 '3R'은 처음부터 또다시 시작되는 것이다.

웹 사이트가 개설되었을 때, 매달 백여 명의 사람들이 그 사이트에 가입했다. 지금은 95만 명이 넘는 회원이 있으며, 북크로싱의 책들은 전 세계로 뻗어 나가는 중이다. 북크로싱은 당신의 독서 경험을 다른 사람들과 나누는 재미있는 방법이다.

구문 해설

2행 He didn't want to **see** the books [(*that*[*which*]) he loved] **become** dusty on his shelf.

▶ see(지각동사) + 목적어 + 동사원형: ~이 …하는 것을 보다

▶ he 앞에 the books를 선행사로 하는 목적격 관계대명사 that[which]이 생략됨

3행 His goal was **to "make** the whole world a library" *so that* people *could* share their books for free.

(S) (V) (C)

▶ to make 이하는 be동사(was)의 보어로 쓰인 to부정사구

▶ so that ~ can ...: ~이 …할 수 있도록 (목적)

7행 Now the fun of reading doesn't end when the book

(S) (V)

does.

▶ does는 반복을 피하기 위해 동사 ends를 대신해 쓰인 대동사

10행 The book is then given an ID number, **which** is put on the inside cover of the book.

▶ which는 an ID number를 선행사로 하는 계속적 용법의 관계대명사 (= and it)

17행 Bookcrossing is a fun way **to *share*** your experience of reading *with* others.

▶ to share는 a fun way를 수식하는 형용사적 용법의 to부정사

▶ share A with B: A를 B와 나누다[공유하다]

UNIT 06.
Art

READING 1   p. 32~33

WORD CHECK

1. sparkle   2. remedy   3. feel like   4. last
5. characteristic

▶ mood: the way that a location or a work of art appears or makes one feel

정답

1. b   2. b   3. Because the light didn't last.   4. b
5. a   6. characteristics, mixed, light, method

해석

보고 싶은 테오에게

방금 너의 다정한 편지를 받았다. 네가 얘기해 준 것들에 대해 매우 고맙게 생각한다. 오늘은 좀 쉬고 있어서 답장 쓸 기회가 생겼단다.

내 그림들에 관해 물었더구나. 너도 알다시피, 나는 늘 각 계절이 지닌 독특한 특징에 관심이 많았어. 음, 지금은 가을이라 숲이 독특한 색들을 드러내고 있단다. 나는 자연의 아름다움에 감탄하며 온종일 나무들 사이에 앉아 시간을 보냈어. 모든 색을 다 칠해 보려 했지만, 힘든 일이더구나. 땅은 아주 짙은 색이지만 그것을 칠하기 위해 커다란 흰색 튜브 물감을 하나 반이나 썼지. 그 흰색을 빨간색, 노란색, 갈색, 검은색과 섞었어. 그랬더니 포도주의 색과 같은 암적색이 되었어. 빛을 받아 밝게 빛나는 싱그러운풀도 있더구나. 그것은 색칠하기가 아주 까다로웠어.

나는 그림을 그리면서 속으로 말했어. 이 가을 저녁의 신비로운 분위기를 그림에 담아내기 전까진 멈춰서는 안 된다고 말이야. 하지만 빛이 계속 있는 게 아니라서 강렬한 붓 터치 몇 번으로 재빨리 그려야만 했어.

나는 최선을 다해 작업을 계속할 거야. 내 건강에 관해 물었는데, 네 건강은 어떠니? 내 생각에 내 치료법이 너에게도 도움이 될 것 같구나. 야외로 나가서 그림을 그리는 것이지. 나는 몸이 피곤할 때조차도 계속 그렇게 하고 싶더구나.

네가 행복하고 건강하길 바란다.

너를 사랑하는 형,
빈센트가

구문 해설

9행 I **spent** a whole day **sitting** among the trees, *admiring* the beauty of nature.

▶ spend + 시간 + v-ing: ~하면서 시간을 보내다

▶ admiring 이하는 동시동작을 나타내는 분사구문

13행 There was also some fresh grass [which caught the light and sparkled brightly].

18행 I will continue to work **as hard as** I **can**.

▶ as + 형용사/부사의 원급 + as + 주어 + can: 가능한 한 ~한[하게] (= as + 형용사/부사의 원급 + as possible)

19행 I think (that) my remedy would help you, too: to be outside, **painting**.

▶ painting: '~하면서'의 의미로 동시동작을 나타내는 분사구문

19행 Even when I'm tired, I still **feel like doing** it.

▶ feel like v-ing: ~을 하고 싶다

▶ it = being outside, painting

WORD FOCUS   color

a light color 연한 색 / a vivid color 선명한 색상 / mix colors 색을 섞다 / add color (to) 색채를 가미하다

WORD CHECK

1. real-life   2. beast   3. rebel   4. familiar
5. recreate
▶ anger: to make sb upset

정답

1. b   2. Because Fauve artists were viewed as rebels during their time.   3. d   4. c   5. ⓓ   6. movement, surprised, unnatural, emotions, express

해석

20세기 초에, 많은 화가들이 전통으로부터 벗어나기 시작했다. 이 시기의 현대 미술 운동 중 하나는 야수파로, 이것은 1904년 프랑스에서 발전하기 시작했다. 'Fauvism'이란 용어는 프랑스 단어 *fauve*에서 왔는데, 이것은 '야수'를 의미한다. 야수파 화가들이 활동하던 당시 그들이 반항아로 여겨졌기 때문에 이 이름이 선택되었을 것이다. 그들의 예술은 보는 이들에게 충격을 주었고, 심지어 분노를 불러일으켰다. 그것은 사람들이 '옳다'고 생각하는 것을 가져다가 '틀리게' 보이도록 만들었다.

앙리 마티스는 이 운동의 창시자 중 한 명이었다. 다른 야수파 화가들과 마찬가지로, 그는 친숙한 형태들을 그것들과 자연스럽게 어울리지 않는 색으로 칠했다. 다시 말해, 풍경화와 초상화들을 '틀린' 색들로 칠했는데 이 색들은 보통 선명하고 독특했다. 전통적으로, 화가들은 대상을 선택해 그것을 대상의 실제 색을 써서 채색하곤 했다. 그러나 마티스는 형태가 색을 결정지어서는 안 된다고 생각했다. 사물을 단순히 현실에서 보이는 것처럼 만드는 대신, 그는 그림에 자신의 느낌을 나타내기 위해 색을 사용했다. 그의 표현에 따르자면, "내가 초록색을 칠할 때, 그것은 잔디가 아니다. 내가 파란색을 칠할 때, 그것은 하늘이 아니다."

〈콜리우르의 열린 창문〉이라는 그림은 마티스의 색의 사용을 보여 주는 훌륭한 예이다. 물이 파란색이 아니라 분홍 색상이고, 벽이 서로 다른 색이기 때문에 그 풍경은 자연스러워 보이지 않는다. 그러나 그 색들은 마티스가 어느 여름날 오후에 느낀 흥분을 표현하는데, 이것이 그가 재현하고자 했던 바였다. 마티스가 색에 관해서는 '옳은 것' 또는 '틀린 것'이 없다고 생각했던 이유가 그 때문이다. 다른 야수파 화가들처럼, 그는 화가가 선택하는 색들은 화가의 창조적인 비전을 표현하기 때문에 그것들이 항상 옳다고 믿었다.

구문 해설

4행   This name **may have been** chosen because Fauve artists *were viewed as* rebels during their time.
▶ may have p.p.: ~했을지도 모른다 (과거에 대한 약한 추측)
▶ 'view A as B(A를 B로 간주하다)'가 수동태로 쓰인 구문

5행   **It** took something [that people considered "right"]

and made **it** look "wrong."
▶ 첫 번째 It은 앞 문장의 Their art를, 두 번째 it은 something that people considered "right"을 가리킴

7행   **Along with** other Fauve artists, he painted familiar forms in colors [that didn't match *them* naturally].
▶ along with: ~와 마찬가지로
▶ them은 앞의 familiar forms를 가리킴

20행   Like other Fauve artists, he believed that the colors [(**that**[**which**]) an artist chooses] are always right ....
▶ the colors를 선행사로 하는 목적격 관계대명사 that[which]이 생략됨

WORD REVIEW TEST

UNIT 05   p. 36

1. d   2. a   3. d   4. b   5. b   6. c   7. a   8. registered
9. public   10. educational   11. remote   12. expand
13. encourage   14. organization   15. process

UNIT 06   p. 37

1. d   2. d   3. c   4. c   5. b   6. a   7. c   8. chance
9. reality   10. familiar   11. characteristics
12. portrait   13. modern   14. subject   15. admire

UNIT 07.
Technology

READING 1   p. 38~39

WORD FOCUS   purpose

object 목적, 목표 / aim 목표, 목적 / intention 의도, 목적 / goal 목표

WORD CHECK

1. sneak   2. prevent   3. standard   4. private
5. encrypt
▶ additional: more than required or expected; extra

정답

1. a   2. Because other users can sneak into the

browsing process and steal your valuable information when HTTP is used.　3. (1) T (2) F　4. c　5. c
6. (1) ⓐ (2) ⓑ (3) ⓑ

해석

　　당신이 웹 사이트를 방문할 때, 당신의 웹 브라우저의 주소창 앞부분에서 'http' 혹은 'https'를 볼 수 있다. 이 글자들은 무엇을 의미할까? 그리고 그것의 목적은 무엇일까? HTTP는 하이퍼텍스트 전송 규약을 나타낸다. 그것은 웹 브라우저와 서버 간에 정보를 교환하는 표준 방식이다. HTTP는 인터넷 사용자들이 문자, 이미지, 동영상을 포함한 모든 종류의 콘텐츠에 접근할 수 있게 한다. 문제는 HTTP를 이용하는 것이 언제나 안전한 것은 아니라는 것이다. HTTP가 사용될 때 다른 사용자들이 검색 과정에 몰래 들어가 당신의 소중한 정보를 훔칠 수 있다. 그것이 바로 안전한 버전인 HTTPS가 만들어진 이유이다.

　　HTTPS는 서버와 브라우저 사이에 안전한 암호화된 연결을 사용함으로써 웹 검색을 더 안전하게 만든다. 다른 사용자들은 이러한 연결을 통해 전달되는 정보를 볼 수 없기 때문에, HTTPS는 당신의 정보를 비밀로 지켜준다. 게다가, HTTPS는 해커가 요청된 정보를 다른 해로운 정보로 바꾸는 것을 막는다. 해커들은 또한 데이터가 암호화되어 있기 때문에 훔칠 수 없을 것이다.

　　그것의 부가적인 안전성 때문에, 대부분의 주요 웹 사이트들은 현재 HTTPS를 사용하고 있다. 그리고 구글 크롬과 같은 인기 있는 웹 브라우저들은 이것을 권장하고 있다. 이제, 어떤 웹 사이트가 HTTPS를 사용한다면, 크롬은 당신의 정보가 안전하다는 것을 알려주기 위해 자물쇠 아이콘을 인터넷 주소창의 앞부분에 보여 준다. 그러나, 어떤 사이트가 HTTP를 사용한다면, 그것은 '안전하지 않음'이라는 경고 메시지를 대신 보여 준다. HTTPS는 당신이 어떤 브라우저를 사용하든지 간에 웹을 더 안전하게 만들고 있다. 따라서 당신이 온라인에 접속할 때마다, 'S'가 보이는지 확인하라!

구문 해설

5행　It is the standard way **to exchange** information

　　between a web browser *and* a server.
　　▶ to exchange는 the standard way를 수식하는 형용사적 용법의 to부정사
　　▶ between A and B: A와 B 사이에

8행　The problem is [**that** *using HTTP* is not always safe].
　　▶ that이 이끄는 명사절이 be동사(is)의 보어로 쓰임
　　▶ that이 이끄는 명사절 안에서 동명사구인 using HTTP가 주어로 쓰임

10행　**That's why** HTTPS, a secure version, was created.
　　▶ that's why: 그것이 ~한 이유이다

13행　In addition, HTTPS **prevents** hackers **from** *replacing* requested data *with* other, harmful data.
　　▶ prevent + 목적어 + from v-ing: ~이 …하는 것을 막다
　　▶ replace A with B: A를 B로 바꾸다[교체하다]

20행　HTTPS is **making** the web **safer**, *no matter what browser* you use.
　　▶ make + 목적어 + 형용사: ~을 …하게 만들다
　　▶ no matter what + 명사: 무슨 ~라도 (= whatever + 명사)

READING 2　　　　p. 40~41

WORD CHECK

1. locate　2. tissue　3. radiation　4. tumor
5. overcome
▶ undergo: to experience sth difficult or unpleasant

정답

1. d　2. d　3. The recovery time of patients is shorter (with the CyberKnife).　4. d　5. b　6. radiation, harm, growth, surgery, recovery

해석

어떤 종류의 칼이 실제로는 칼이 아닐까?

　　정답은 '사이버나이프'이다. 사이버나이프 로봇 방사선 수술 시스템은 종양이 있는 사람들을 치료하기 위해 의사들에 의해 사용되고 있는 첨단 장비이다.

　　종양의 위치가 확인되면 사이버나이프는 환자에게 고통을 주지 않고 종양을 파괴하기 시작하는 고에너지 방사선을 쏜다. 그것은 로봇 팔에 붙어 있는데, 이것이 사이버나이프가 환자의 어떤 움직임에도 자동으로 조절되도록 돕는다. 그것은 폐나 척추, 뇌를 포함한 신체 어느 부위에도 사용될 수 있다.

　　사이버나이프는 매우 정밀하여 주변 조직을 훼손하지 않고 종양을 제거할 수 있다. 이것은 의사들이 기존의 수술로는 도달할 수 없었던 곳에 있는 종양도 치료할 수 있도록 해준다. 종양이 즉시 없어지는 것은 아니지만, 사이버나이프는 종양이 커지는 것을 막고 서서히 그 크기를 감소시킨다.

　　사이버나이프를 이용하면 환자의 회복기도 더 단축된다. 이 때문에 사이버나이프는 몸이 너무 약해 기존 형태의 수술을 견뎌내지 못하는 사람들에게 좋은 대안이 된다. 이것은 신속히 끝나서, 환자들이 당일 퇴원하는 경우도 종종 있다. 대체로, 이것은 기존의 수술보다 훨씬 스트레스가 적다.

　　전 세계적으로 수백 개 병원에 설치된 사이버나이프 로봇 방사선 수술 시스템을 통해 이미 수만 명의 환자가 이 방식으로 종양을 치료받았다. 암은 극복하기 어려운 질병이지만, 사이버나이프 같은 첨단 기술이 사람들에게 희망을 주고 있다.

구문 해설

1행　The CyberKnife Robotic Radiosurgery System is high-tech equipment [being used by doctors **to treat** people with tumors].
　　▶ to treat은 목적을 나타내는 부사적 용법의 to부정사

This makes it a good option for people [who are **too** weak **to undergo** traditional kinds of surgery].

▶ too ~ to-v: 너무 ~해서 …할 수 없는

16행 Tens of thousands of patients have already **had** their tumors **treated** in this fashion, ...

▶ have + 목적어 + p.p.: ~이 …되도록 하다

UNIT 08.
Biology

READING 1   p. 42~43

WORD FOCUS   method

an effective method 효과적인 방법 / a reliable method 믿을 수 있는 방법 / provide a method 방법을 제공하다 / develop a method 방법을 개발하다

WORD CHECK

1. decrease   2. rare   3. impurity   4. chemical
5. wound

▶ encounter: to come into contact with sb or sth

정답

1. c   2. It begins to clot as soon as it encounters any type of impurity.   3. ⓒ   4. b   5. c   6. clots, drugs, obtain, return

해석

투구게는 놀라운 생물체이다. 그들은 2억 5천만 년이 넘도록 거의 변하지 않았다. 오늘날 투구게는 과학자들에게 희귀하고 값진 물질을 제공해주는데, 바로 그들의 푸른 피이다.

보통의 붉은 피에는 철분이 포함되어 있지만, 투구게의 피는 구리를 포함하고 있기 때문에 푸른색이다. 그러나 이것이 그들의 피를 아주 유용하게 만드는 것은 아니다. 대신, 그들의 피가 응고하는 방식이 그렇다. 응고는 피가 걸쭉해져서 고형의 물질을 형성할 때 일어난다. 이것은 베인 상처나 다친 부위로부터 피가 흐르는 것을 멈추게 하기 위해 이뤄진다. 투구게의 피는 어떠한 종류의 불순물을 만나는 즉시 응고되기 시작한다.

미국의 과학자 프레더릭 뱅은 1950년대에 투구게의 피를 가지고 실험을 시작했다. 그는 곧 Limulus amebocyte lysate 또는 LAL이라고 알려진, 응고를 일으키는 화학 물질을 발견했다. 그 당시에는 약의 불순물을 검사할 좋은 방법이 없었다. 그러나 뱅은 LAL이 이런 목적으로 사용될 수 있다는 것을 깨달았다. 오늘날 미국에서 LAL은 모든 의약품이 인체용으로 승인을 받기 전에 그것을 검사하는 데에 쓰인다.

LAL은 극도도 희귀하고 리터당 15,000달러만큼이나 값이 나갈 수 있다. LAL의 합성 형태는 투구게의 피 없이 생산될 수 있는데, 현재 이용 가능하다. 그러나 제약 회사들은 투구게의 피에서 발견되는 LAL로부터 (합성 LAL로) 변경하는 데 꾸물거려왔다. 그 종을 보존하기 위해서, 과학자들은 게를 살아있는 상태로 바다에 돌려보내기 전에 각 게로부터 약 3분의 1의 혈액만을 추출한다. 이것에도 불구하고, 매년 수천 마리의 투구게가 피 추출 과정에서 죽는다. 바라건대, 합성 LAL이 더 널리 사용되면서, 이 숫자는 감소할 것이다.

구문 해설

6행 **This**, however, is not *what* makes their blood so
S ... V ... C
useful.

▶ This는 바로 앞 문장의 내용을 가리킴

▶ 관계대명사 what이 이끄는 절이 문장에서 보어 역할을 함

8행 Instead, **it** is *the way* it clots.

▶ 첫 번째 it은 앞 문장의 what makes their blood so useful을, 두 번째 it은 their blood를 가리킴

▶ the way 뒤에 관계부사 how가 생략된 형태임 (the way와 how는 둘 중 하나만 사용함)

13행 He soon discovered the chemical [**that** causes the clotting], [**known** as Limulus amebocyte lysate, or LAL].

▶ that이 이끄는 주격 관계대명사절과 known이 이끄는 과거분사구가 동시에 the chemical을 수식

15행 Today, LAL is used in America **to check** all drugs before they are approved for human use.

▶ to check는 목적을 나타내는 부사적 용법의 to부정사

18행 However, pharmaceutical companies have been slow to **make the switch** from the LAL [found in horseshoe crab blood].

▶ make the switch: 변경하다

READING 2   p. 44~45

WORD FOCUS   gather

assemble 모이다, 모으다 / congregate 모이다 / flock (많은 수가) 모이다 / get together 모이다, 만나다

WORD CHECK

1. jail   2. blood transfusion   3. murder   4. survive
5. inject

▶ make sure: to check so that no doubt remains about sth's certainty

정답

1. b   2. d   3. (1) T (2) F (3) F (4) T   4. ⓓ-ⓑ-ⓒ-ⓐ
5. experimented, sicker, continued, types, safer

해석

혈액은행이 왜 있는지 아는가? 그것은 돈을 저축하기 위한 것이 아니다. 그것은 생명을 구하기 위한 것이다. 만일 누군가 사고를 당해 많은 피를 흘린다면, 의사는 수혈해줌으로써 그 사람을 도울 수 있다.

이 모든 것이 아주 간단하게 들리지만, 오늘날의 수혈은 300년 이상에 걸친 실험의 결과물이다. 1667년, 몇몇 영국 과학자들이 한 실험을 지켜보기 위해 모였다. 한 남자가 자신의 팔에 피를 주입하는 것에 동의한 상태였다. 그 개념은 오늘날의 수혈과 비슷했지만 한 가지 중요한 차이점이 있었는데, 그 피가 양의 피라는 것이었다! 이 남자는 살아남았지만 또 다른 남자는 파리에서 유사한 실험 이후 사망했다. 관련 의사는 살인죄로 감옥에 갈 뻔했으며, 1678년에 프랑스 정부는 모든 수혈을 금지했다.

그러나 영국에서는 수혈 실험이 계속되었고, 1840년경에 의사들은 사람과 사람 간의 수혈을 시행하고 있었다. 하지만 안타깝게도 이러한 수혈은 이따금 사람들을 더 아프게 만들었다. 마침내, 1901년에 카를 란트슈타이너라는 오스트리아 의사가 이에 대한 원인을 밝혀냈는데 그것은 바로 혈액형이었다. 그는 사람의 피에는 A형, B형, AB형, O형과 같이 네 가지의 주된 유형이 있다는 것을 알아냈다. O형 환자가 수혈이 필요하다면 의사는 그 환자가 반드시 O형 피를 수혈받도록 해야 한다. 이 발견 이후로 수혈은 훨씬 더 안전해졌고 이제는 매년 수천 명의 생명을 구한다.

구문 해설

[2행] ..., doctors can help that person **by giving** him or her a blood transfusion.
　　▶ by v-ing: ~함으로써

[6행] A man had **agreed to** *have* some blood *injected* into his arm.
　　▶ agree to-v: ~하기로 동의하다
　　▶ have + 목적어 + p.p.: ~이 …되도록 하다

[8행] The doctor **involved** *was* nearly *sent to jail* for murder, ...
　　▶ involved: '관련된'이라는 의미로 주로 명사를 뒤에서 수식함
　　▶ be sent to jail: 감옥에 보내지다

WORD REVIEW TEST

UNIT 07   p. 46

1. a   2. d   3. a   4. d   5. b   6. a   7. c   8. replaced
9. access   10. overcome   11. connection   12. harm
13. option   14. recovery   15. request

UNIT 08   p. 47

1. c   2. a   3. d   4. b   5. c   6. a   7. b   8. clot
9. survive   10. transfusion   11. injected
12. experiment   13. approve   14. synthetic
15. continue

UNIT 09.
Sports

READING 1   p. 48~49

WORD FOCUS   specific

vague 모호한, 희미한 / ambiguous 애매모호한 / fuzzy 애매한, 불분명한 / imprecise 부정확한, 애매한

WORD CHECK

1. entirely   2. challenge   3. strict   4. improper
5. official
▶ prestige: the high status that sb or sth achieves through success in society

정답

1. a   2. (1) T (2) F   3. b   4. Because the soles were orange-colored.   5. c   6. prestigious, white, improper, change

해석

1877년에 시작되어, 윔블던 선수권 대회(줄여서 '윔블던')는 세계에서 가장 오래된 테니스 대회이다. 오늘날, 그것은 호주 오픈, 프랑스 오픈, 미국 오픈과 함께 4개의 '그랜드 슬램' 테니스 대회 중 하나이다. 그러나, 윔블던은 그중에서도 가장 권위 있는 것으로 알려져 있다. 그것은 또한 엄격한 복장 규정으로도 알려져 있다.

오랫동안, 윔블던의 복장 규정은 선수들이 거의 전부 흰옷을 입도록 요구해 왔다. 테니스를 치는 동안 흰옷을 입는 전통은 1870년대까지 거슬러 올라갈 수 있는데, 그때는 땀 흘리는 것이 부적절하다고 여겨졌다. 테니스 선수들은 땀을 덜 흘리도록 흰옷을 입고는 했는데, 그것이 다른 색깔들보다 그들을 더 시원하게 해주었다.

많은 선수들이 그 복장 규정에 도전해 왔다. 예전 최고 순위의 선수 안드레 아가시는 화려한 의상을 좋아했는데, 1988년부터 1990년까지 그 대회에서 경기를 하는 것을 거부했다. 몇몇 다른 최고의 선수들은 색깔이 있는 옷을 입은 것으로 관계자들로부터 경고를 받았고 언론의 집중을 받았다. 세리나 윌리엄스는 2010년과 2012년에 그녀의 치마 속에 밝은색의 반바지를 입었다. 2013년, 로저 페더러는 밑창이 주황색이었기 때문에 그의 신발을 바꾸라는 말을 들었다!

2014년에, 매우 구체적인 일련의 규칙들이 도입되었다. 이 규칙들은 목둘레선과 소맷동과 같은 몇 곳에는 흰색이 아닌 색깔들이 허용되지만, 오직 '1센티미터보다 넓지 않은 한 줄의 테두리'만 허용된다는 것을 분명히 했다. 이 규칙은 또한 머리띠, 양말, 신발, 그리고 심지어 선수들의 속옷에도 적용된다!

윔블던의 복장 규정은 너무 엄격한 것으로 비판을 받아 왔다. 그러나, 그 대회의 역사와 명성은 그것을 정말로 특별하게 만들도록 돕는다. 이러한 이유로, 그 복장 규정은 당분간 바뀔 것 같지 않다.

구문 해설

[10행] The tradition of wearing white while playing tennis
(S)
can be traced back to the 1870s, **when** sweating was
(V)
considered improper.
▶ when은 계속적 용법으로 쓰인 관계부사 (= and at that time)

[15행] Some other top players **have been warned** by officials *for wearing* colored garments and (**have**) **received** media attention.
▶ 현재완료 수동태와 현재완료 구문으로 been warned와 received는 병렬 관계임
▶ wearing은 전치사 for의 목적어로 쓰인 동명사

[25행] However, the tournament's history and prestige **help** *make* it truly *special*.
▶ help (to)-v: ~하도록 돕다
▶ make + 목적어 + 형용사: ~이 …하게 만들다

READING 2   p. 50~51

WORD FOCUS   essential

important 중요한 / necessary 필요한, 불가피한 / crucial 중대한, 결정적인 / significant 중요한, 소중한

WORD CHECK

1. resolve   2. appropriate   3. popularity   4. delay
5. toss
▶ employ: to give sb a job and pay for it

정답

1. a   2. b   3. d   4. A mediator watches the game and helps to make a decision if the two teams cannot resolve a disagreement.   5. b   6. (1) ⓒ (2) ⓐ (3) ⓑ (4) ⓓ

해석

당신은 프리스비 원반이 단지 당신의 친구들과 던지기를 위한 것으로 생각할지도 모른다. 그러나 많은 나라들에서, 그것은 '얼티미트'라고 불리는 흥미로운 팀 경기를 하는 데 사용된다. 얼티미트는 1960년대에 미국에서 만들어졌다. 그러나 그것은 전 세계적으로 인기를 얻고 있다. 오늘날에는, 심지어 정기적으로 개최되는 많은 국제 선수권 대회도 있다.

얼티미트는 각 7명인 두 팀을 필요로 한다. 그리고 그것은 양 끝에 엔드 존이 있는 직사각형의 경기장에서 행해진다. 선수들은 다른 팀의 엔드 존 쪽으로 원반을 옮기기 위해서 자신의 팀원들에게 그것을 패스한다. 원반을 들고 있는 선수는 그것을 가지고 달릴 수 없다. 또한, 그들은 원반을 잡은 지 10초 안에 다른 선수에게 재빨리 패스해야 한다. 한 선수가 적합한 엔드 존 안에서 원반을 잡을 때, 그 선수의 팀은 1점을 얻는다. 경기는 한 팀이 미리 정해진 점수(보통 15점)에 이를 때 끝난다.

얼티미트의 한 가지 흥미로운 측면은 평상시의 심판의 부재이다. 반칙을 선언하고 그들 사이의 의견 충돌을 해결하는 것은 바로 선수들이다. 따라서, 좋은 스포츠맨 정신은 필수적이다. 모든 선수들은 서로를 공평하고 정중하게 대해야 한다. 이러한 공정성과 존중의 환경은 '경기의 정신'으로 알려져 있다.

경우에 따라서는, 경기를 보며 양 팀이 의견 불일치를 해결할 수 없을 때 결정을 도와주는 중재자가 있다. 그리고 몇몇 프로 리그들은 지연을 막기 위해 심판들을 고용하기도 한다. 그러나 얼티미트의 모든 경기에서, 가장 중요한 것은 '경기의 정신'이 유지되는 것이다.

구문 해설

[6행] Today, there are even many international championships [held regularly].

[10행] The player [holding the disc] cannot run with it.

[15행] **It** is the players **who** call fouls and resolve any disagreements among themselves.
▶ It ~ that[who] 강조구문으로, the players를 강조 (강조하는 것이 사람일 때 that 대신 who를 쓸 수 있음)

[19행] In some cases, there is a mediator [**who** watches the game and *helps to* **make** a **decision** if the two teams cannot resolve a disagreement].
▶ who 이하는 a mediator를 선행사로 하는 주격 관계대명사절
▶ help to-v: ~하도록 돕다
▶ make a decision: 결정하다

[20행] And some professional leagues **do** employ referees in order to prevent delays.
▶ 동사의 의미를 강조하기 위해 동사 employ 앞에 조동사 do가 쓰임

UNIT 10.
History

WORD FOCUS mistake

a silly mistake 어리석은 실수 / a common mistake 흔한 실수 / make a mistake 실수하다 / admit one's mistake ~의 실수를 인정하다

WORD CHECK

1. purchase 2. resource 3. fur 4. separate
5. glacier
▶ nickname: to give sb or sth a new, informal name

정답

1. c 2. Because Alaska[it] was considered too far away for any Russians to live there. 3. a 4. c 5. a 6. largest, sold, waste, resources

해석

 알래스카는 미국의 일부이지만, 캐나다에 의해 본토에서 분리되어 있다. 그럼에도 불구하고 알래스카는 미국에서 가장 큰 주로, 미국 나머지 지역의 5분의 1 크기이다. 이 주는 거대한 빙하들과 북미에서 가장 높은 매킨리산을 비롯한 눈 쌓인 산들로 뒤덮여 있다. 해마다 수천 명의 관광객이 하이킹과 사냥을 하고, 그곳의 뛰어난 자연미를 경험하러 알래스카로 여행을 간다.

 러시아 탐험가들이 1741년에 알래스카를 발견했고, 곧 러시아의 모피 상인들이 알래스카 주변 바다에서 해달을 사냥하기 시작했다. 그들은 또한 몇몇 군사 기지와 마을을 세웠다. 그러나 알래스카는 러시아인들이 살기에는 너무 멀리 떨어져 있다고 여겨졌다. 결국 러시아는 1867년에 알래스카를 미국에 팔았다. 720만 달러에 팔렸으니 이 거대한 주가 에이커당 불과 2센트밖에 되지 않았던 것이다.

 그것의 놀랍도록 낮은 가격에도 불구하고, 많은 미국인은 이 매입이 엄청난 실수라고 생각했다. 신문들은 그 매입을 진행했던 윌리엄 헨리 수어드 국무장관의 이름을 따서 이 새로운 곳을 '수어드의 아이스박스'라고 불렀다. 하지만 이후의 발견들은 알래스카가 자원의 보고임을 입증했다. 1896년에 그곳에서 금이 발견되자 수천 명이 부자가 되려고 그곳으로 이주했다. 이 주는 또한 관광객이 방문하기에 흥미로운 곳일 뿐만 아니라 연어, 목재, 그리고 석유의 풍부한 원천이다. 한때 '수어드의 아이스박스'라고 불렸던 이 주가 지금은 미국에서 가장 풍요롭고 아름다운 장소 중 하나이다.

구문 해설

(4행) ..., **one fifth** the size of the rest of the country.
 ▶ one fifth(= 1/5): 분수의 분자는 기수로, 분모는 서수로 표현

(12행) ..., Alaska was considered **too** far away *for any Russians* **to live** there.
 ▶ too ~ to-v: 너무 ~해서 …할 수 없다
 ▶ for any Russians는 to live의 의미상의 주어

(16행) Newspapers **nicknamed** the new area "Seward's Icebox" **after** the Secretary ... Seward, ...
 (A) the new area (B) "Seward's Icebox" (C) the Secretary ... Seward
 ▶ nickname A B after C: C의 이름을 따서 A의 별명을 B라고 짓다

(18행) But later discoveries **proved** Alaska **to be** full of resources.
 ▶ prove + 목적어 + to-v: ~이 …임을 입증하다

(20행) The state is also a rich source of salmon, lumber, and oil, **as well as** an interesting place for tourists *to visit*.
 (A) a rich source of salmon, lumber, and oil (B) an interesting place for tourists
 ▶ A as well as B: B뿐만 아니라 A도
 ▶ to visit은 an interesting place를 수식하는 형용사적 용법의 to부정사

정답

1. a 2. c 3. the fourth square 4. b 5. b
6. b, c, f

해석

국제 적십자

 제2차 이탈리아 독립 전쟁이 한창이던 1859년, 솔페리노 전투가 북부 이탈리아에서 벌어졌다. 그것은 9시간 지속되었고 결국 수만 명의 병사가 죽거나 부상당했다. 이것은 군대의 의료팀이 돌보기에는 너무 많은 숫자였다. 그 전투가 일어났을 때, 앙리 뒤낭이라는 스위스의 한 사업가가 그 지역을 여행하고 있었고, 그는 병사들의 고통에 큰 충격을 받았다.

 몇 년 후에 그는 그가 목격한 것에 관한 책을 썼다. 그의 책에서 그는 모든 군대는 양측의 부상병들을 도울 수 있는 자원 의사와 간호사를 동반해야 한다고 제안했다. 이듬해 공익협회라는 한 스위스 단체가 뒤낭의 제안을 논의하기 위해 회의를 열었다. 그들은 뒤낭을 포함하여 다섯 명으로 구성된 위원회를 설립했다. 이 위원회가 국제 적십자의 시작이었다.

 1864년에 유럽 국가들과 브라질, 멕시코, 그리고 미국의 대표들이 '전장에 있는 군대 부상자의 상태 개선에 대한 제네바 협약'에 서명하기 위해 스위스에 모였다. 이 협약은 적십자 자원봉사자들이 해를 입지 않고 전장에 들어갈 수 있도록 하는 규약을 확립했다. 마침내 이 규약들은 국제법으로 인정되었다.

 조직 내 지도자들과의 갈등 때문에 뒤낭은 나중에 그 조직에서 쫓겨났다. 1901년에 최초의 노벨 평화상을 받았음에도 불구하고, 1910년 세

상을 떠날 당시에 그는 거의 잊힌 상태였다. 그러나 그가 시작한 단체는 세계로 퍼져 나갔다. 오늘날 그것은 거의 모든 나라에 지부를 두고 있고 9천만 명 이상의 직원과 자원봉사자가 국제 적십자 및 그와 관련된 단체에서 일하고 있다.

구문 해설

6행 In his book, he **suggested** {*that* all armies **should be** accompanied by volunteer doctors and nurses [who could help ... from both sides]}.
▶ 요구 · 명령 · 제안 등을 나타내는 동사 뒤에 이어지는 that절의 동사는 「(should) + 동사원형」으로 씀

8행 The next year a Swiss organization [called the Public Welfare Association] held a meeting **to discuss** Dunant's proposal.
▶ to discuss는 목적을 나타내는 부사적 용법의 to부정사

13행 It established rules [that would **allow** Red Cross volunteers **to enter** battlefields *without being harmed*].
▶ allow + 목적어 + to-v: ~이 …하도록 해 주다
▶ without v-ing: ~하지 않고

WORD REVIEW TEST

UNIT 09 p. 56

1. c   2. d   3. a   4. a   5. d   6. b   7. a   8. c
9. absence   10. fairness   11. improper   12. strict
13. essential   14. prestigious   15. introduce
16. disagreement

UNIT 10 p. 57

1. b   2. d   3. b   4. d   5. c   6. b   7. a   8. resource
9. mainland   10. branch   11. nicknamed   12. fort
13. explorer   14. accompany   15. representative

UNIT 11.
Culture

READING 1 p. 58~59

WORD FOCUS complex

complicated 복잡한 / intricate 복잡한 / sophisticated 정교한, 복잡한

WORD CHECK

1. settle   2. blend   3. reputation   4. instrument
5. slave
▶ modern: in the style of the current time

정답

1. a   2. They brought stringed instruments and European music (to the Americas).   3. c   4. b
5. (1) F (2) T   6. (1) settlers (2) drums (3) complicated (4) beat (5) solo

해석

　　음악과 춤은 라틴 아메리카 문화에서 큰 역할을 한다. 그 음악은 그 지역의 토착 문화, 유럽, 그리고 아프리카의 전통적인 양식들이 혼합된 것이다. 그것은 스페인 사람들이 현악기와 유럽의 음악을 아메리카 대륙으로 가져왔을 때 시작되었다. 나중에, 아프리카 노예들은 북과 자신들의 음악을 가져왔다.

　　살사는 라틴 음악에서 가장 인기 있는 양식 중 하나인데, 그것의 빠른 박자와 복잡한 리듬으로 알려져 있다. 살사 춤은 당신의 다리와 엉덩이를 경쾌한 음악의 박자에 맞춰 움직이는 것을 포함하는데, 이 또한 인기가 있다. 살사의 기원은 쿠바 음악에서 찾을 수 있다. 제2차 세계 대전 이후, 많은 쿠바 사람들이 뉴욕시로 이주했다. 그들은 스페니시 할렘이라 불리는 동네에 정착했다. 그곳에서, 그들의 음악은 다른 이민자들의 음악과 섞였다. 1960년대에 이르러, 현대 살사가 생겨났다.

　　라틴 음악의 또 다른 인기 있는 형태는 삼바이다. 그것은 원래 19세기에 브라질에서 생겼다. 삼바는 현악기, 금관 악기, 그리고 북으로 연주된다. 살사와 마찬가지로, 그것 역시 춤을 포함한다. 전통적인 브라질 삼바 춤은 단독으로 공연된다. 그러나, 볼룸 삼바는 커플들에 의해 춰지는데, 다른 나라에서 더 인기가 있다. 과거에, 삼바는 그것이 가난한 동네에서 자주 공연되었다는 사실 때문에 평판이 좋지 않았다. 그래서 사람들은 '삼바 학교'라고 불리는 클럽을 만들기 시작했다. 이 학교들은 그들이 축제에서 삼바 춤을 공연하면서 인기를 얻었다. 서서히 삼바는 더욱 품위 있는 공연이 되었다.

　　라틴 아메리카의 음악과 춤에는 많은 다른 형태들이 있다. 그것들은 보사노바, 메렝게, 룸바, 그리고 탱고를 포함한다. 그것들 모두는 다른 문화들의 혼합이고 전 세계의 사람들로부터 사랑을 받는다.

5행 Salsa is **one of the most** popular **styles** of Latin music, known for its fast tempo and complex rhythms.
- ▶ one of the + 최상급 + 복수명사: 가장 ~한 … 중 하나

9행 From there, their music mixed with **that** of other immigrants.
- ▶ that은 앞에 언급된 music을 가리킴

15행 In the past, samba had a bad reputation **due to** the fact *that* it was often performed in poor neighborhoods.
- ▶ due to: ~ 때문에
- ▶ that이 이끄는 절은 the fact와 동격 관계

READING 2
p. 60~61

WORD FOCUS preserve

abandon 버리다, 포기하다 / lose 잃다, 지키지 못하다 / destroy 파괴하다, 말살하다 / ruin 망치다

WORD CHECK

1. application   2. approval   3. diversity   4. regulate
5. tease
- ▶ approximately: around a certain number or amount

정답

1. d   2. b   3. b   4. Because they believe it has a negative effect on diversity and fails to embrace the modern trend of globalism.   5. c   6. (1) government (2) gender (3) church (4) preserve (5) embrace

해석

당신은 부모들이 그들의 자녀에게 어떠한 이름이든 골라줄 권리가 있다고 생각할지도 모른다. 그러나, 이것은 항상 그런 것은 아니다. 세계의 많은 나라들은 아이들의 작명을 규제하는 법을 가지고 있다. 이러한 나라들 중 하나는 덴마크이다. 덴마크의 부모들은 정부가 승인한 명단에서 이름을 골라야 한다. 그 이름은 아이의 성별을 분명하게 보여 줘야만 한다. 그것은 또한 그 목록에 보이는 대로 철자가 정확하게 쓰여야 한다. 따라서, 덴마크의 부모들은 그들의 딸 이름을 카밀라(Camilla)라고 지을 수 있지만, 카밀라(Cammilla)는 허용되지 않을 것이다.

그러나, 부모들이 그 목록에 없는 이름을 사용하기를 원한다면 따를 수 있는 절차가 있다. 그들은 그들의 지역 교회로부터 승인을 받는 것부터 시작해야 한다. 그 후에, 그 요청은 정부로 보내진다. 정부는 연간 약 1,000개의 신청서를 받는다. 그러나 정부는 그것들 중 약 20%를 거절한다. 결국 이름이 승인될지라도, 그 과정은 수개월이 걸릴 수 있다.

이 정책은 불공평하고 불필요하게 보일 수 있다. 그러나 정부가 아이들에게 특이한 이름을 주는 것을 어렵게 만드는 데는 이유가 있다. 첫 번째 이유는 아이들 자신을 보호하기 위해서이다. 이상한 이름을 가진 아이들은 종종 그들의 반 친구들에게 놀림을 받는다. 또 다른 이유는 덴마크의 문화유산을 지키기 위해서이다. 그 나라는 덴마크의 역사에 걸쳐 사용되어 온 전통적인 이름들과 철자들을 보존하기 위해 노력하고 있다.

이러한 이유들에도 불구하고, 많은 사람들은 그 정책에 반대한다. 그들은 그것이 다양성에 부정적인 영향을 미치고 세계화라는 현대적 추세를 포용하지 못한다고 믿는다. 이에 대응하여, 덴마크 정부는 그 법을 덜 엄격하게 만들었는데, 목록에 있는 이름의 수를 7,000개에서 33,000개로 늘렸다.

3행 Many countries around the world have laws [**that** regulate the naming of children].
- ▶ that은 laws를 선행사로 하는 주격 관계대명사

13행 Even if the name **ends up** *being* approved, the process can take months.
- ▶ end up + v-ing: 결국 ~하게 되다
- ▶ being approved는 end up의 목적어로 쓰인 동명사구

15행 The government, however, has reasons for **making** *it* difficult *to give* children unusual names.
- ▶ making은 전치사 for의 목적어로 쓰인 동명사
- ▶ it은 가목적어, to give 이하가 진목적어

18행 The country is **trying to preserve** the traditional names and spellings [that *have been used* …].
- ▶ try to-v: ~하기 위해 애쓰다[노력하다]
- ▶ have been used는 '사용되어 왔다'라는 뜻의 현재완료 수동태

21행 In response, the Danish government has made the law less strict, **increasing** *the number of* names on the list from 7,000 names to 33,000.
- ▶ increasing 이하는 부대상황을 나타내는 분사구문
- ▶ the number of: ~의 수

UNIT 12.
Psychology

READING 1
p. 62~63

WORD FOCUS   enhance

reduce 줄이다, 축소하다 / weaken 약화시키다 / lessen (크기 ·
강도 · 중요도 등을) 줄이다

WORD CHECK

1. repetitive   2. trigger   3. autonomous
4. concentrate   5. equipment
▶ tingle: a feeling like many pins or needles touching the
skin

정답

1. c   2. a   3. They report feeling a pleasurable tingle
in their heads that travels down the backs of their necks.
4. b   5. (1) T (2) F (3) T   6. tingling, repeated,
touching, relax, depressed

해석

　　딱딱한 표면 위를 두드리는 손톱이나 물웅덩이에 떨어지는 물방울을
상상해 보라. 이러한 소리들은 당신이 어떤 기분이 들게 하는가? 많은 사람
들에게, 그것들은 행복이나 휴식의 감정을 자아낸다. 이러한 종류의 경험은
ASMR이라고 불린다. 그것은 '자동 감각 쾌락 반응'을 나타낸다. 몇 년 동
안 사람들은 그것을 치료의 한 종류로 사용해 왔다. 그들은 종종 그 효과를
높이기 위해서 최첨단의 장비로 소리들을 녹음하고 듣는다. 요즘, 그것은 온
라인에 게시된 무료 영상들을 통해 인기를 얻게 되었다.

　　ASMR 소리를 듣는 사람들은 종종 목덜미를 타고 내려오는 기분 좋은
얼얼함을 그들의 머리에서 느낀다고 보고한다. 이러한 느낌들을 만들어내
는 그 소리들은 방아쇠라고 불린다. 가장 일반적인 청각 ASMR 방아쇠들
중 몇몇은 속삭임, 긁음, 또는 다양한 표면들을 두드리는 것을 포함한다. 청
각 방아쇠와 함께, 시각 그리고 촉각과 관계된 방아쇠들도 있다. 시각적 방
아쇠의 측면에서는, 반복적인 손의 움직임이 흔하다. 촉각에 관련한 방아쇠
에 관해서는, 장난감 슬라임을 가지고 노는 것이 포함된다. 어떤 사람들은
일부 방아쇠에 반응하지만 다른 것들에는 반응하지 않는다. 그리고 다른 사
람들은 어떤 것에도 전혀 반응하지 않는다.

　　방아쇠에 반응하는 사람들은 다양한 목적으로 ASMR을 사용한다. 그
것은 사람들이 잠이 들게 하거나 그들의 일에 집중하는 것을 도울 수 있다.
사람들은 또한 스트레스를 덜 느끼고 더 편안함을 느낄 수 있다. 심지어 우
울증으로 고통받는 사람들도 ASMR을 들은 후에 기분이 나아지는 것을
경험할 수 있다.

　　ASMR에 대한 관심이 급격하게 증가하고 있지만, 여전히 그것이 어
떻게 작용하는지를 완전히 이해할 수 있는 충분한 과학적 연구가 없었다.
미래에는, 정신 건강 전문가들이 그들의 환자들 중 일부를 치료하기 위해

ASMR을 이용할 수 있을 가능성이 있다.

구문 해설

1행 Imagine fingernails [**tapping** on a hard surface] or
drops of water [**falling** into a puddle].
▶ tapping ... surface와 falling 이하는 각각 fingernails와
drops of water를 수식하는 현재분사구

10행 People [**listening** to ASMR sounds] often report
feeling a pleasurable tingle in their heads [**that** travels
down the backs of their necks].
▶ listening ... sounds는 People을 수식하는 현재분사구
▶ feeling은 동사 report의 목적어로 쓰인 동명사
▶ that은 a pleasurable tingle을 선행사로 하는 주격 관계대
명사

15행 Some people respond to some triggers **but not to
others**.
▶ but not to others = but they do not respond to
other triggers

21행 Although interest in ASMR is growing rapidly, there
still hasn't been enough scientific research **to fully
understand** [*how* it works].
▶ to fully understand 이하는 enough scientific
research를 수식하는 형용사적 용법의 to부정사
▶ how 이하는 간접의문문으로 「의문사 + 주어 + 동사」의 어순이
며, understand의 목적어로 쓰임

READING 2
p. 64~65

WORD FOCUS   firm

resolute 단호한, 확고한 / definite 확실한, 확고한 /
determined 단단히 결심한, 완강한

WORD CHECK

1. confident   2. tackle   3. hesitate   4. intuition
5. reversible
▶ rating: a grade, such as a number, that shows an
evaluation of sth

정답

1. b   2. It can prevent us from choosing without
careful thought.   3. b   4. b   5. carefully, frustration,
perfect, intuition, important

해석

당신은 친구들을 만나러 나갈 때 무엇을 입을지 결정하는 데 어려움을 겪는가? 당신은 두 개의 새로운 스마트폰 모델 사이에서 결정을 할 수 없을 때 꼼짝 못 하게 되는가? 그렇다면, 당신은 아마도 우유부단함으로 고군분투하고 있는지도 모른다.

망설임은 당신이 신중한 생각 없이 선택하는 것을 막아줄 때 좋은 것이 될 수 있다. 그러나, 당신이 너무 오래 망설인다면, 그것은 좌절과 기회를 놓치는 것으로 이어질 수 있다. 우유부단함은 종종 완벽주의에 의해 일어난다. 사람들이 실수하는 것이나 실패의 가능성에 대해 너무 걱정할 때, 그들은 어떤 결정도 내릴 수 없게 된다.

다행히도, 불필요한 망설임을 피하기 위해 당신이 따를 수 있는 몇 가지 조언들이 있다. 이러한 조언들은 당신이 더욱 자신감 있는 의사결정자가 되도록 도와줄 것이다. 첫째, 당신의 직감을 따르는 것이 도움이 될 수 있다. 과도하게 분석하지 않기 위해서는, 당신의 선택지들을 적어 보아라. 그러고 나서 빠르게 각 선택지에 1부터 10까지의 점수를 매겨라. 그런 다음 단순하게 가장 높은 점수를 가진 선택지를 골라라.

당신은 또한 점심으로 무엇을 먹을지와 같은 사소한 일에도 당신의 의사결정을 연습할 수 있다. 작은 일들에 빠르고, 확실한 결정을 잘 할 수 있게 되면, 당신은 필요할 때 중요한 결정들을 다루는 데 더 능숙해질 것이다.

마지막으로, 많은 결정들이 보이는 것만큼 중요하지 않다는 것을 인정하는 것이 도움이 될 수 있다. 그냥 스스로에게 물어보아라, "이 결정이 10년 후에 중요할 것인가?" 만약 답이 그렇다고 해도, 많은 결정들은 되돌릴 수 있다는 것을 기억하라. 예를 들어, 당신이 미술 수업에 등록하기로 결정했는데 결국 당신은 그것을 즐기지 않는다는 것을 알게 되었다면, 당신은 그냥 그만둘 수 있다. 새로운 것을 시도하는 데 따르는 위험은 보통 그렇게 크지 않다.

구문 해설

[1행] Do you find **it** difficult **to decide** *what to wear* **when** (you are) going out *to meet* your friends?

▶ it은 가목적어, to decide 이하가 진목적어
▶ what to-v: 무엇을 ∼할지
▶ when 이하는 접속사가 생략되지 않은 분사구문
▶ to meet은 목적을 나타내는 부사적 용법의 to부정사

[20행] Finally, **it** can be helpful **to acknowledge** [*that* many decisions are**n't as** important **as** they seem].

▶ it은 가주어, to acknowledge 이하가 진주어
▶ 접속사 that 이하는 acknowledge의 목적어 역할
▶ not as + 형용사/부사의 원급 + as: ∼만큼 …하지 않은[않게]

[22행] For example, if you decide to enroll in an art class **only to find** [*that* you don't enjoy it], you can just quit.

▶ only to-v: 결국 ∼하다
▶ 접속사 that 이하는 동사 find의 목적어 역할

WORD REVIEW TEST

UNIT 11   p. 66

1. a   2. c   3. a   4. b   5. c   6. a   7. d   8. b
9. diversity   10. unusual   11. performed   12. region
13. annually   14. origin   15. involve   16. complex

UNIT 12   p. 67

1. a   2. d   3. b   4. a   5. a   6. d   7. b   8. c
9. relaxed   10. frustration   11. equipment
12. struggling with   13. enhance   14. avoid
15. possibility   16. decision

UNIT 13.
Animals

READING 1   p. 68~69

WORD FOCUS   tiny

small (크기 · 수) 등이 작은 / little (크기 · 규모가) 작은 / minute 극히 작은

WORD CHECK

1. distance   2. flight   3. purpose   4. waterproof
5. attract
▶ broad: great in size across the sides of sth

정답

1. d   2. d   3. They have thick, oily feathers (that keep them warm and dry while they swim in icy water).   4. c
5. waterproof, connected, broad, warmth, attract

해석

새를 생각할 때, 우리는 흔히 그것들이 상공을 우아하게 나는 모습을 상상한다. 모든 새가 실제로 날 수 있는 건 아니지만, 모든 새는 날개가 있다. 그러나 날개는 새에게만 있는 특징이 아니다. 곤충과 박쥐에게도 날개가 있다. 하지만 깃털은 어떤가? 모든 새는 깃털이 있으며, 깃털은 새에게서만 찾아볼 수 있다.

깃털은 가능한 한 가볍도록 설계되어 있다. 그러나 동시에 매우 튼튼하며 방수가 된다. 깃털을 자세히 들여다보면, 당신은 그것이 수천 개의 작은 부분들로 이루어져 있다는 것을 알게 될 것이다. 이 부분들은 한 개의 깃털에서 백만 군데 이상 결합되어 있다. 새의 날개에는 깃털들이 부분적으로 서로를 덮고 있어 공기가 전혀 통과하지 못 한다. 이는 비행을 가능하게 해

주고 새를 따뜻하게 해 준다.

하지만 모든 새의 깃털이 똑같은 것은 아니다. 예를 들어, 앨버트로스는 먼 거리를 날 수 있게 해 주는 튼튼하고 폭이 넓은 깃털을 가지고 있다. 반면에, 펭귄은 차가운 물속을 헤엄치는 동안 그들을 따뜻하고 마른 상태로 유지해 주는 두껍고 기름기 있는 깃털을 가지고 있다.

새들은 또한 그들의 깃털을 여러 가지 목적으로 사용한다. 예를 들어, 몇몇 새들은 알을 품는 동안 알을 따뜻하게 유지하기 위해 깃털을 사용한다. 그리고 어떤 새들은 그들의 주변 환경과 같은 색의 깃털을 가지고 있는데, 이것은 그들이 적으로부터 숨을 수 있게 돕는다. 공작과 같은 다른 새들은 매우 밝고 화려한 깃털을 가지고 있으며 그들은 짝을 유인하는 데 깃털을 사용한다.

모든 새의 깃털은 그들이 어디에서 어떻게 사느냐에 따라 다르다. 이 깃털들이 종종 아름답게 보일지라도 그것들은 새의 각 종(種)의 생존에 있어 항시 필수적이다.

구문 해설

2행 **Not all** birds can actually fly, but all birds have wings.
▶ not all ~: 모두 ~인 것은 아니다 (부분 부정)

8행 Feathers are designed to be **as light as possible**.
▶ as ~ as possible: 가능한 한 ~한

13행 For example, albatrosses have strong, broad feathers [that **allow** them **to fly** long distances].
▶ allow + 목적어 + to-v: ~이 …하도록 해 주다

18행 And some have feathers [that are **the same** color **as** their environment]; ....
▶ the same ~ as ...: …와 같은 ~

READING 2 · p. 70~71

WORD CHECK

1. feed on 2. paddle 3. grab 4. incredible
5. freshwater
▶ angle: the direction in relation to a surface

정답

1. a 2. b 3. Because it allows the fish to be sure of the bird's actual position. 4. c 5. c 6. freshwater, daily, strategy, angle, unusual

해석

호수 위로 낮게 나는 새는 물속에 위험한 것이 도사리고 있다고 생각하지 않을지도 모른다. 이 때문에 새는 물고기가 갑자기 튀어 올라 자신을 잡는 순간 놀라는 것이다! 과학자들은 최근에 이것이 제비들이 남아프리카 공화국의 슈로다 댐 호수 위를 날 때 일어나는 일임을 발견했다.

이 새들을 사냥하는 물고기는 아프리카 타이거피시다. 전 세계에서 새를 먹이로 하는 민물고기는 약 다섯 종에 불과하다. 이 물고기들의 대부분은 새가 물에 빠지거나 그들 바로 위의 수면에서 헤엄치며 돌아다닐 때만 이렇게 한다. 그러나 아프리카 타이거피시는 정기적으로 제비를 사냥한다. 사실상, 그들은 매일 그렇게 한다. 이것은 아마 슈로다 댐 호수에 타이거피시가 먹을 만한 다른 먹이가 많지 않기 때문일 것이다.

과학자들은 타이거피시가 발전시킨 엄청난 사냥 능력에 놀란다. 타이거피시는 호수 위로 날고 있는 제비를 발견하면, 물 표면 가까이나 더 깊은 물 아래에서 헤엄을 쳐서 그 새를 쫓아간다. 그것은 새를 추월할 때까지 속도를 낸다. 그러고 나서 빛이 대기에서 물로 들어올 때 빛의 각도가 어떻게 변하는지를 고려한다. 이것은 그 물고기가 새의 실제 위치를 확신하도록 해 준다. 최종적으로, 타이거피시는 물 밖으로 튀어 올라 그것의 날카로운 이빨로 공중에서 제비를 잡아챈다.

이것은 대부분의 먹이 사슬에서 일어나는 일과 정반대이다. 새가 물고기를 사냥하는 것이 훨씬 더 일반적이기 때문에, 타이거피시가 제비를 먹이로 한다는 사실은 정말로 보기 드문 일이다.

구문 해설

1행 A bird [flying low over a lake] may not think there is **anything dangerous** in the water.
▶ -thing으로 끝나는 (대)명사는 형용사가 뒤에서 수식

3행 ... this is **what** happens to barn swallows *as* they fly over the Schroda Dam lake in South Africa.
▶ what은 선행사를 포함하는 관계대명사
▶ as는 '~할 때'라는 의미로 쓰인 접속사

9행 ... because there isn't much other food *for tigerfish* **to eat** in the Schroda Dam lake.
▶ to eat은 much other food를 수식하는 형용사적 용법의 to부정사이고, for tigerfish는 to부정사의 의미상의 주어

18행 Since **it** is much more common *for birds* **to hunt** fish, the fact *that* tigerfish feed on barn swallows is quite extraordinary.
▶ it은 가주어, to hunt fish가 진주어, for birds는 to부정사의 의미상의 주어
▶ that ... swallows는 the fact와 동격 관계

UNIT 14.
Origins

WORD FOCUS   narrow

broad 폭이 넓은, 광대한 / wide 넓은, 너른 / extensive 넓은, 광범위한

WORD CHECK

1. theorize   2. magician   3. evidence   4. flow out
5. row
▶ perform: to entertain others by acting, playing music, etc.

정답

1. b   2. They believed it could cure fevers and other illnesses.   3. c   4. d   5. (1) ⓐ (2) ⓓ (3) ⓒ (4) ⓑ

해석

　'아브라카다브라'라는 말은 여러 언어 사용자들에게 친숙하다. 요즘에 이 말은 주로 마술사들이 사용한다. 그들은 마술 묘기를 부릴 때 이 '마법의' 말을 한다. 그러나 고대에는 사람들이 이 말의 위력에 대해서 좀 더 진지했다. 그들은 그것이 열과 다른 질병들을 치료할 수 있다고 믿었다.

　아브라카다브라에 관한 최초의 알려진 언급은 세레누스 사모니쿠스라는 로마 의사에게서 비롯되었다. 서기 2세기에, 그는 〈De Medicina Praecepta〉라는 시를 썼다. 그 시는 병자들이 그들의 목에 둘렀던 부적에 대해 말한다. 부적 안에는 특별한 단어가 쓰인 종잇조각이 있었다.

　그 단어는 11번 쓰였는데, 매번 마지막 철자가 없어졌다. 최종적으로, 11번째 행에는 'A' 하나만 남게 되었다. 그 부적은 삼각형 모양이었다. 사람들은 아브라카다브라라는 말과 함께, 이 삼각형이 몸에서 병을 몰아낼 수 있다고 여겼다. 병은 폭이 넓은 맨 윗부분으로 들어와서 좁은 바닥을 통해 흘러 나간다. 일단 (병이) 나가면, 그것은 삼각형의 좁은 바닥으로 다시 들어올 수 없다.

　이 부적에 대한 설명이 아브라카다브라라는 말에 대한 최초의 기록된 증거이긴 하지만, 많은 사람은 그 말이 훨씬 더 오래되었다는 이론을 내세운다. 어떤 사람들은 그것이 고대 히브리어인 압, 벤, 그리고 루아치 카데시에서 유래한 것이라고 여기는데, 이는 '성부, 성자, 그리고 성령'이라는 뜻이다. 다른 사람들은 그것이 ('내가 말하는 대로 창조하리라'라는 뜻의 아브라케다브라에서 비롯된) 아람어에서 왔다고도 하고, 그럼에도 또 다른 이들은 그 말이 칼데아어라고 주장한다. 정답은 역사 속에 묻혀 있고 아마도 끝내 밝혀지지 않을 것이다. 그러나 한 가지는 확실한데, 아브라카다브라는 마술사들이 그들의 마법 지팡이를 흔들 때 사용되는 말 그 이상이라는 점이다.

구문 해설

10행　The poem tells of an amulet [**that** sick people wore around their necks].
　▶ that은 an amulet을 선행사로 하는 목적격 관계대명사

10행　Inside the amulet was a piece of paper with the special word [written on it].
　　　　부사구 　　　V　　　　S
　▶ 부사구가 강조되어 앞으로 나오면서 주어와 동사가 도치됨

16행　**Once** (*the illness was*) gone, it could not ....
　▶ Once ~: 일단 ~하면
　▶ 부사절의 주어가 주절의 주어와 같은 경우 「부사절의 주어 + be동사」는 생략 가능

18행　..., but many people theorize that it is **even** older.
　▶ even: 훨씬 (비교급 강조)

WORD FOCUS   career

pursue a career 경력을 추구하다 / a long career 오랜 경력 / a successful career 성공적인 경력 / a promising career 유망한 직업

WORD CHECK

1. pension   2. laboratory   3. lecture   4. field
5. contribution
▶ broadcast: to send out programs on TV or radio

정답

1. c   2. d   3. b   4. d   5. c   6. annually, scientific, understandable, educate, attract

해석

　영국 왕립연구소 크리스마스 강연은 180여 년 전에 영국에서 시작되었다. 강연은 매년 12월 연휴 기간 동안 런던에서 열리는데, 이는 학생들이 더 쉽게 강연에 참석하도록 한다. 강연은 과학에 관한 것이고 그 분야의 전문가들에 의해 행해지지만, 이해하기 아주 쉬워서 심지어 어린 학생들도 즐길 수 있다.

　이 강연은 원래 1825년에 마이클 패러데이라는 영국의 한 과학자에 의해 제안되었다. 그 당시에, 패러데이는 영국 왕립연구소에서 연구실 책임자로 재직 중이었다. 그는 너무 가난해서 정식으로 학교에 다니지 못하는 아이들을 교육하는 데 관심이 있었다. 패러데이 자신도 가난한 집안 출신이었기에 제대로 된 교육을 받는 데 어려움을 겪었다. 과학자인 험프리 데이비의 강연에 영감을 받아, 패러데이는 어린 나이에 과학에 전념했다. 시간이 지나면서 그는 그 분야에 많은 공헌을 했고, 정부로부터 집과 연금을 제의받는 영예를 누렸다. 그는 그 제의를 거절하였지만, 자기 자신의 경험을 떠올

리고는 한 가지를 요청했는데 가난한 아이들이 교육의 기회를 제공받아야 한다는 것이었다. 그렇게 해서 크리스마스 강연이 탄생하였다.

크리스마스 강연은 많은 사람이 과학 분야의 직업을 고려해 보도록 고무했다. 수학자 마커스 드 사토이는 2006년에 강연을 했는데 그는 12살 때 크리스마스 강연에 따라갔었다. 그가 과학자가 되기로 결심하게 만든 것은 바로 그 경험이었다.

오늘날, 크리스마스 강연은 세계적인 행사가 되었다. 강연들은 한국을 포함한 여러 나라에서 방송되었다. 그것들은 이제 온라인으로도 볼 수 있다. 당신이 과학에 관심이 있든 없든 간에, 하나 들어 보는 게 어떤가?

구문 해설

8행　... children [who were **too** poor **to attend** school regularly].
▶ too ~ to-v: 너무 ~해서 …할 수 없는

11행　..., Faraday **dedicated himself to** science at an early age.
▶ dedicate oneself to: ~에 헌신[전념]하다

16행　The Christmas Lectures have **inspired** many people **to consider** careers in the field of science.
▶ inspire + 목적어 + to-v: ~이 …하도록 고무하다

18행　**It** was that experience **that** *made* him *decide* to become a scientist.
▶ It ~ that ... 강조구문으로, that experience를 강조
▶ make(사역동사) + 목적어 + 동사원형: ~이 …하게 만들다

23행　**Whether** you are interested in science **or not**, *why not consider* listening to one?
▶ whether ~ or not: ~이든 아니든
▶ why not + 동사원형 ~?: ~하는 게 어때?

WORD REVIEW TEST

1. c   2. a   3. d   4. c   5. a   6. c   7. b   8. angle
9. species   10. extraordinary   11. flight   12. closely
13. opposite   14. actual   15. spot

1. d   2. c   3. c   4. d   5. a   6. b   7. c   8. a
9. d   10. b   11. c   12. ancient   13. honor
14. recall   15. dedicate

UNIT 15.
Economics

READING 1　　　　　　　　　　　p. 78~79

WORD FOCUS　pleasurable

enjoyable 즐거운 / delightful 기분 좋은, 마음에 드는 / entertaining 재미있는, 즐거움을 주는 / satisfying 만족스러운

WORD CHECK

1. possess   2. ruin   3. expectation   4. show off
5. motivation
▶ ignore: to pay no attention to sth or sb

정답

1. a   2. c   3. c   4. b   5. It can help marketers understand the motivations of modern consumers and easily persuade them to purchase products.
6. (1) value (2) unusual (3) physical (4) experience
(5) preserve

해석

오늘날, 사람들은 자신의 육체적 필요뿐만 아니라 심리적 필요 또한 충족시키기 위해서 소비한다. 예를 들면, 새로운 스마트폰을 고를 때, 많은 사람들은 그것의 기능들은 무시한다. 그들은 단순히 유명한 브랜드를 고른다. 이 경우, 그들이 소비하는 것은 제품 그 자체가 아니라 브랜드라는 개념이다. 이것은 개념적 소비로 알려져 있다.

개념적 소비에는 몇 가지 종류가 있다. 첫 번째는 기대를 포함하는데 우리는 어떤 것을 살 때, 그것의 가치에 대한 기대를 가진다는 것이다. 한 실험에서, 사람들이 저렴한 와인보다는 비싼 와인을 마시고 있다고 생각할 때 뇌의 쾌락 중추들이 더 활동적이었다. 그러나, 사실 둘 다 똑같은 저렴한 와인이었다. 이것은 사람들의 기대가 그들의 소비 경험이 얼마나 즐거운지에 영향을 줄 수 있다는 것을 보여 준다.

개념적 소비의 두 번째 유형은 경험을 포함한다. 사람들은 다른 사람들에게 과시할 수 있는 새롭고 흥미로운 경험을 갖고 싶어 한다. 이런 종류의 경험 추구는 왜 일부 사람들이 고급 호텔보다는 얼음으로 만들어진 호텔에 머무르는 것을 선택하는지 설명한다. 그들은 우수한 개념적 경험을 즐기기 위해서 열등한 육체적 경험을 흔쾌히 받아들인다.

기억의 소비는 마지막 유형이다. 사람들은 때때로 어떤 경험에 대한 기억을 경험 그 자체보다 더 가치 있게 여긴다. 예를 들면, 레스토랑에서 훌륭한 식사를 한 커플은 두 번째 식사를 위해 결코 돌아오지 않을지도 모른다. 왜냐하면 그들은 두 번째 방문이 그들의 첫 번째 경험의 특별한 기억을 망칠 수 있다고 걱정하기 때문이다. 이것은 개념들이 때로는 우리가 더 많이 소비하기보다는 더 적게 소비하도록 장려한다는 것을 보여 준다.

개념적 소비에 대해 배우는 것은 마케팅 담당자들이 현대 소비자들의 동기를 이해하고 그들이 제품을 구매하도록 쉽게 설득하는 것을 도울 수 있다.

구문 해설

[10행] This shows (**that**) people's expectations can affect [*how* pleasurable their experience of consuming is].

▶ 접속사 that이 생략되었으며, that 이하는 동사 shows의 목적어로 쓰임

▶ how 이하는 형용사를 포함하는 간접의문문으로 「how + 형용사 + 주어 + 동사」의 어순

[12행] People want to possess new and interesting experiences [(**that**[**which**]) they can *show off* to others].

▶ new and interesting experiences를 선행사로 하는 목적격 관계대명사 that[which]이 생략됨

▶ show off: 과시하다

[13행] This kind of experience-seeking explains {**why** some people choose to stay in a hotel [*made* of ice] **rather than** a fancy hotel}.

▶ why가 이끄는 절이 동사 explains의 목적어로 쓰임

▶ made of ice는 a hotel을 수식하는 과거분사구

▶ A rather than B: B라기 보다는 A

[23행] Learning about conceptual consumption can **help** marketers ┌ **understand** ...
│ and
└ easily ***persuade*** them *to purchase* ....

▶ help + 목적어 + (to)-v: ~이 …하도록 돕다

▶ persuade + 목적어 + to-v: ~이 …하도록 설득하다

| **READING 2** | **TOEFL** | p. 80~81 |

정답

1. d 2. the second square 3. b 4. a 5. d
6. b, c, f

해석

세계은행

제2차 세계 대전 중에 유럽의 많은 나라가 대규모의 피해를 입었다. 전쟁이 끝난 후, 그들은 도시를 재건하고 경기를 회복하기 위한 도움이 필요했다. 세계은행은 이 국가들에게 돈을 빌려줌으로써 그들을 원조하기 위해 1944년에 창설되었다.

오늘날 유럽 경제는 튼튼하지만, 세계은행은 여전히 활동하고 있다. 그것은 이제 개발 도상국에 돈을 빌려주고 있는데, 저금리 또는 무이자 차관을 제공한다. 이 차관으로, 개발 도상국은 경제를 재건하고 개선할 수 있다. 이는 도움이 되는데 부유한 정부들이 대출을 해줄 때 보통 매우 높은 이자율을 고집하기 때문이다. 세계은행은 또한 빈곤한 나라들에 15년에서 20년까지의 더 긴 상환 기간을 준다.

세계은행은 또한 더 직접적인 방법으로 개발 도상국을 돕고 있다. 일부 단체들이 단순히 가난한 나라에 식량을 주는 데 반해, 세계은행은 더 장기적인 해결책으로 교육을 활용한다. 세계은행은 농부들이 더 많은 식량을 재배할 수 있도록 그들이 새로운 농사 기술을 배우게 돕는다. 이 방법으로 모든 사람에게 더 많은 식량이 생길 것이고, 농부들도 더 나은 삶을 살게 될 것이다. 그 결과, 그들은 경제에 환원할 더 많은 돈을 벌게 될 것이다.

게다가, 세계은행은 질병으로 인한 고통을 없애기 위해 노력한다. 전반적인 건강 상태를 개선하기 위해 개발 도상국들은 의사와 간호사를 필요로 한다. 세계은행은 지역 정부가 사람들이 의료 교육을 받을 수 있는 기회를 창출하는 것을 돕는다. 이렇게 해서 더 많은 의사와 간호사가 아픈 사람들을 도울 수 있다.

하지만 이 기구는 그것이 지원하기로 한 프로젝트들 때문에 일부 비판에 직면한다. 예를 들어, 1981년 브라질에서 세계은행이 자금을 지원한 개발 프로그램은 열대 우림의 파괴를 가중시켰다. 또한, 힘이 강한 나라들이 의사 결정 과정을 독식하게 하여, 그 조치들에 가장 직접적인 영향을 받는 나라들의 목소리를 종종 무시하는 결과를 낳기도 한다.

구문 해설

[5행] ..., **providing** them **with** low-interest or interest-free loans.

▶ provide A with B: A에게 B를 제공하다

[12행] As a result, they will have more money **to put back** into the economy.

▶ to put back은 more money를 수식하는 형용사적 용법의 to부정사

[15행] ... create opportunities *for people* **to get** a medical education.

▶ to get은 opportunities를 수식하는 형용사적 용법의 to부정사이고, for people은 to부정사(to get)의 의미상의 주어

[17행] ..., face some criticism for the projects [(**that**[**which**]) it chooses to support].

▶ the projects를 선행사로 하는 목적격 관계대명사 that[which]이 생략됨

[19행] Also, it **allows** powerful countries **to dominate** its decision-making process, often *ignoring* voices from the nations [most directly affected by its actions].

▶ allow + 목적어 + to-v: ~이 …하도록 해 주다

▶ ignoring 이하는 부대상황을 나타내는 분사구문

WORD REVIEW TEST

UNIT 15   p. 82

1. a 2. d 3. a 4. a 5. c 6. a 7. b 8. ignored
9. persuaded 10. destruction 11. expectations
12. inferior 13. consume 14. rebuild 15. interest

READING
EXPERT